BB

French

talk 2

Sue Purcell

Series Editor: Alwena Lamping

BBC Active, an imprint of Educational Publishers LLP, part of the Pearson Education Group, Edinburgh Gate, Harlow, Essex CM20 2JE, England

© Educational Publishers LLP 2007

ISBN 978-1-4066-1287-5

Cover design: adapted from original artwork by Helen Williams and Matt Bookman
Cover photograph: © Danita Delimont / Alamy
Insides design: Nicolle Thomas, Rob Lian
Layout: eMC Design www.emcdesign.org.uk
Illustrations © Tim Marrs @ Central Illustration Agency
Commissioning editor: Debbie Marshall
Development editor: Jenny Gwynne
Project editor: Melanie Kramers
Marketing: Fiona Griffiths, Paul East
Senior production controller: Man Fai Lau

Audio producer: Martin Williamson, Prolingua Productions
Sound engineer: Dave Morritt at Studio AVP
Presenters: Juliet Dante, Framboise Gommendy, Yves Aubert, Jean-Pierre Blanchard

Printed and bound in China. (CTPSC/01)

The Publisher's policy is to use paper manufactured from sustainable forests.

Contents

Introduction

Talk French 2 is a new course from BBC Active, helping you to improve your French in an enjoyable and stimulating way. It's designed for people who have some experience of French – whether from an introductory course (such as the bestselling **Talk French**), a first-level class or time spent in France – and who want to build on what they've learnt.

Recognising that language is reinforced through repetition, **Talk French 2** takes time to revisit the basics, as well as taking you forward at a sensible and manageable pace. The course deals with interesting, adult topics such as food and wine, getting to know people, finding out about French property, shopping and coping with problems. It's ideal, whether you want to learn for work or for fun, and as preparation for a national Level 1 qualification. The course covers the preliminary level of the Languages Ladder.

What makes **Talk French 2** special?
- It has been developed by a team of professionals with extensive experience in adult language learning.
- The carefully designed activities focus on all the dimensions of learning French, and aim to develop your ability to speak the language, understand replies, and experiment with reading and writing in French.
- It recognises that, in order to go beyond basic phrases and really express yourself, you'll need to know some French grammar. And it presents the grammar in a way that's easy to understand, without jargon or complex technical explanations.
- It incorporates highly effective learning strategies, such as predicting, educated guesswork, memory building, gist reading and selective use of a glossary.
- Its structured and systematic approach promotes steady progress and a real sense of achievement, boosting your confidence as well as your linguistic ability.

Talk French 2, which includes this book and 140 minutes of audio recordings by native French speakers, is an interactive course, involving you at all the stages of the learning process.

Wherever you see this: **1•5**, the phrases or dialogues are recorded on the CD (i.e. CD1, track 5).

It consists of:

Units 1 to 10, each containing:

- *En France*, an insight into French culture to set your learning in context;
- summaries of key language for you to listen to, read and repeat to practise your pronunciation;
- activities designed around the audio recordings, to develop your listening skills and understanding;
- succinct *En français* explanations of how the language works, placed exactly where you need the information (where appropriate, these are expanded in the grammar section at the back - see links e.g. **G15**);
- a *Put it all together* section, consolidating what you've learnt before you put it to the test in *Now you're talking*, where you are prompted to speak French;
- a final progress check with a quiz and a checklist summarising key points.

En plus supplements, at regular intervals, which will:

- take you that little bit further, reinforcing and extending what you've learnt in the two preceding units;
- broaden your vocabulary and/or place words that you know into a new context;
- develop your reading and writing skills.

A comprehensive reference section:

- a set of clear definitions of essential grammar terms (on page 6)
- transcripts of all the audio material
- answers to the activities
- a guide to pronunciation and spelling
- a grammar section
- French-English glossary
- English-French glossary.

BBC Active would like to thank all the language tutors who contributed to the planning of the **Talk 2** series. Our particular thanks go to Pam Lander Brinkley MA (Ed) and Sue Maitland, York ACES (Adult and Community Education Service).

Glossary of grammatical terms

To make the most of the *En français* notes, it helps to know the meaning of the following key grammatical terms.

- **Nouns** are the words for people, places, concepts and things: *son, doctor, sheep, house, Scotland, time, freedom.*
- **Gender** Every French noun is either masculine or feminine, as are any articles and adjectives that relate to it.
- **Articles** are *the* (definite article) and *a/an* (indefinite article).
- **Pronouns** avoid the need to repeat nouns: *it, them, you, they.*
- **Singular** means one.
- **Plural** means more than one.
- **Adjectives** describe nouns: *French* wine, the children are *small.*
- **Adverbs** add information to adjectives and verbs: *very* big, to speak *slowly.*
- **Verbs** are words like *to go, to sleep, to eat, to like, to have, to be,* that refer to doing and being.
- **Infinitive** French verbs are listed in a dictionary in the infinitive form, ending in -**er**, -**ir** or -**re**. The English equivalent is *to: to eat, to have.*
- **Regular verbs** follow a predictable pattern, while **irregular verbs** don't – they have to be learnt separately.
- The **person** of a verb indicates who or what is doing something:

  1st person = the speaker: *I* (singular), *we* (plural)

  2nd person = the person(s) being addressed: *you*

  3rd person = who/what is being talked about: *he/she/it/they*
- The **tense** of a verb indicates when something is done:

in the past	perfect tense	*I worked, I have worked*
	imperfect tense	*I was working, I used to work*
now	present tense	*I work, I'm working*
in the future	future tense	*I will work*

- The **subject** of a sentence is the person/thing carrying out the verb: *they* have two children, *Anna* reads the paper.
- The **object** of a sentence is at the receiving end of a verb: they have *two children*, Anna reads *the paper*.

Moi, j'adore la France

getting to know people

giving information about people

talking about work

explaining why you're learning French

En France ...

it's increasingly popular to combine a **séjour linguistique** *language holiday* with an **expérience culturelle**. Look out for opportunities to improve your French while following up another of your interests: you can enjoy French wines on a **stage de dégustation de vin** *wine-tasting course*, learn to cook **à la française** on a **cours de cuisine** *cookery course*, discover **la France profonde** *rural France*, find out about **la littérature**, **l'art** or **l'histoire de l'art**, or test your limits with **sports d'aventure**.

Getting to know people

1   1•2 Listen to the key language:

Comment tu t'appelles?	What's your name?
Comment vous appelez-vous?	What's your name?
Je m'appelle ...	My name is ...
Tu es/Vous êtes d'où?	Where are you from?
Je suis (de) ...	I'm (from) ...
Tu habites/Vous habitez où?	Where do you live?
J'habite en/au/aux/à ...	I live in ... (*country/town*)

2   1•3 At the start of a combined French and wine-tasting course in Avignon, the teacher, rather than introduce herself, invites students to ask her questions. Listen and note her first name and where she lives.

Nom .... *Bouchard*   **Ville** ....

> As people get to know each other better, they use the informal **tu** rather than **vous**. Young people often do this from the start.
> **Tu** and **vous** are followed by different forms of the verb. The **tu** form sounds exactly like the form used with **je**, although in writing it has -s at the end: **j'habite – tu habites**.   **G12**

3   1•4 Listen to students Liam and Sonia getting to know each other. She suggests they use **tu** – **On se dit tu?** Fill the gaps in their conversation.

- Bonjour, je .... Liam.
- ◆ Enchantée, Liam. On se dit tu?
- Oui, d'accord.
- ◆ Tu ...... américain? Anglais?
- Je ...... irlandais. Et toi, comment tu ....?
- ◆ Sonia.
- ...... es d'où?
- ◆ Je suis .... Saint-Pétersbourg, en Russie. Je .... russe. Mais j'habite maintenant .... Allemagne.
- Et moi, j'........... en Angleterre, près ...... Cambridge, avec mon frère.

4   Have a go at introducing yourself. Give your name and nationality; say where you're from and where you live.

Giving information about people

1   1•5 Listen to the key language:

Je vous présente ...	Let me introduce ... to you.
Il/Elle s'appelle ...	His/Her name is ...
Liam est ... Il a ...	Liam is ... He has ...
Ils/Elles habitent ici.	They live here.
Il/Elle a dix ans.	He/She's ten years old.
Ils/Elles ont ...	They have ...

2   1•6 Look again at Liam and Sonia's conversation on page 8 and see if you could introduce them to others (*his brother* is **son frère**). Then listen to how they do it, and compare your versions.

The infinitive of many verbs ends in -er: **habiter, présenter**. The final **-er** is replaced by other endings, depending on who/what is involved. For most verbs, the endings are regular and predictable:

I je	-e	*we* nous	-ons
you tu	-es	*you* vous	-ez
he/she/we il/elle/on	-e	*they* ils/elles	-ent

Only the **nous** and **vous** endings actually sound different.
On means *one* or *you* in a general sense; it's often used instead of **nous** to say *we*: **on a trois enfants** *we've got three children.*   **G13**

3   1•7 Juliette's group ask more questions. Listen and decide whether these facts are true or false. **Sa fille** is *her daughter*, **ses fils** is *her sons*.

		vrai	faux
a	Juliette est mariée.		
b	Son mari s'appelle Christophe.		
c	Ils ont deux enfants.		
d	Sa fille s'appelle Aurélie. Elle est étudiante.		
e	Ses fils s'appellent Pascal et Christophe.		
f	Christophe et Aurélie habitent chez leurs parents.		
g	Son fils Pascal a vingt-quatre ans.		

Now write the correct version of any that are false. You might need the transcript on page 107.

Talking about work

1   1•8 Listen to the key language:

Qu'est-ce que tu fais/vous faites (comme travail)?	What (job) do you do?
Je travaille à/pour ...	I work at/for ...
Je suis ...	I'm a/an ...
Depuis quand?	Since when?
Depuis combien de temps?	How long for?
Depuis 2003/cinq ans.	Since 2003/For five years.

2   1•9 Match these words for jobs to the illustrations, using the glossary if you need to. Then listen to people talking about what they do for a living and tick the jobs you hear mentioned.

serveur/serveuse
mécanicien/mécanicienne
rédacteur/rédactrice
coiffeur/coiffeuse
médecin
journaliste
plombier

En français

To say you've been doing something for a period of time or since a particular time, use **depuis** and a verb in the present tense:

J'<u>habite</u> ici <u>depuis</u> 2005. *I've been living here since 2005.*
J'<u>apprends</u> le français <u>depuis</u> un an. *I've been learning French for a year.*

G13

3   1•10 Listen to Isabel and Aldo and underline the correct option.

- Isabelle has been working as a press officer for a large hospital since 2000 / 2002 / 2003.
- Laurent has been an estate agent for 3 / 13 / 30 years.

4   How would you ask Stéphanie in French what job she does, and how long she's been doing that? If Stéphanie has been a hairdresser for six years, how would she answer your questions?

Explaining why you're learning French

1 1•11 Listen to the key language:

Pourquoi?	Why?
Pour parler avec ...	(In order) to talk to ...
Parce que ...	Because ...
... je voudrais ...	... I'd like to ...
... j'aime bien ...	... I like ...
... j'adore ...	... I love/adore ...
voyager/les langues	travelling/languages

2 1•12 Juliette asks her students why they want to learn French: **Pourquoi est-ce que vous voulez apprendre le français?** Read their replies and match them up with the English translations. Then listen and tick the replies as you hear them. Which one in the list is not mentioned? Listen out for **j'aime beaucoup** *I like very much*.

a J'aime bien voyager.	**1** My friends have a house in France.
b Pour aller en Afrique francophone.	**2** To help my daughter, who's learning French in school.
c Parce que j'aime beaucoup les langues.	**3** I love the bread, the wine and the cheese!
d Moi, j'adore la France!	**4** I'd like to work in France.
e Je voudrais travailler en France.	**5** I like travelling.
f Parce que mes amis ont une maison en France.	**6** To go to French-speaking Africa.
g J'adore le pain, le vin et le fromage!	**7** I like languages a lot.
h Pour aider ma fille, qui apprend le français à l'école.	**8** I work with a French woman.
i Parce que je travaille avec une Française.	**9** I just adore France!

3 1•13 Listen to Anna. Why is she learning French and how long has she been learning it?

4 Using a dictionary if you need to, work out how to say why you're learning French.

put it all together

1 Match the French and the English.

a J'habite en France parce que mon mari est français.	**1** I like working in France.
b Elle s'appelle comment?	**2** How long for?
c Je voudrais travailler en France.	**3** What are their names?
d Nous sommes ici pour apprendre le français.	**4** I'd like to work in France.
e J'aime bien travailler en France.	**5** I live in France because my husband is French.
f Elles s'appellent comment?	**6** What's her name?
g Depuis combien de temps?	**7** We're here to learn French.

2 Add in the correct form of the verbs given below.

aimer	tu		vous		on	
parler	je		elle		ils	
travailler	nous		elles		tu	
habiter	j'		ils		vous	

3 Here's a profile of a graphic designer from Besançon.

Nom Berthès
Prénom Pierre-Yves
Date de naissance
11 décembre 1973
Nationalité Français
Ville Besançon   Depuis 15 ans
Profession graphiste   Depuis 8 ans

a How would he introduce himself? Say his name, age in 2007, nationality; where he lives and how long he's been living there, what job he does and since when.

b How would you introduce him to a group of people?

4 Think of two people you know and practise introducing them.

now you're talking!

1   1•14 You're going to be asked these questions. Answer them as if you were Rachel Moore, who's been working as a chemical engineer for the past seven years. She's learning French because she likes travelling and fancies working in France or Switzerland.

- **Bonjour. Comment vous appelez-vous?**
- **Vous êtes américaine?**
- **Vous êtes d'où en Grande-Bretagne?**
- **Qu'est-ce que vous faites comme travail?**
- **Vous êtes ingénieur chimiste depuis combien de temps?**
- **Pourquoi est-ce que vous voulez apprendre le français?**

> **Nom** Moore
> **Prénom** Rachel
>
> **Nationalité** britannique
> **Ville** Bristol
> **Profession** ingénieur chimiste

2   1•15 Now it's your turn to ask the questions. At a party, you start a conversation with a young couple.

- Say good evening and ask their names.
- ◆ **Moi, je m'appelle Mathieu – Mathieu Garnier – et voici ma femme Amélie.**
- Ask where they live.
- ◆ **On habite à Grenoble.**
- Find out how long they've been living in Grenoble.
- ◆ **Depuis trois ans.**
- Ask what they do for a living.
- ◆ **Moi, je suis graphiste, et Amélie est journaliste. On travaille tous les deux à la maison. C'est pratique parce qu'on a une petite fille.**
- Ask how old she is.
- ◆ **Elle a quatorze mois. Elle est adorable!**

quiz

1 If someone asks **Qu'est-ce que vous faites comme travail?**, what do they want to know?

2 What key word would you search for in a phone directory if you had a burst water pipe?

3 When you're talking about yourself in the present tense, what letter does an **-er** verb generally end in?

4 Which two verb endings in the present tense sound different from the rest?

5 To say your son is 13 years old, do you need **ai**, **a** or **est** to complete this sentence? **Mon fils** ...... **treize ans**.

6 If you've been working in Bath since 1998, what word will you need to add here? **Je travaille à Bath** .... **1998?**

7 What could you add to **j'aime** .... **voyager** to say you like travelling a lot?

8 How do you ask *where* and *why* in French?

Now check whether you can ...

- introduce yourself
- say where you live and what you do for a living
- ... and how long you've been doing these
- explain why you're learning French
- askpeople their name and nationality, where they are from, what they do and where they live
- introduce someone
- provide information about where someone lives and works

Successful language learning needs plenty of practice and it also helps to have a personal angle – it's much easier to remember words that have an immediate relevance to you personally. So, using a dictionary, start to boost your vocabulary by creating as many sentences as you can starting with **je suis**, **j'aime bien**, **j'aime beaucoup**, **j'adore**, **je voudrais**.

On part à quelle heure?

using the 24-hour clock

... and the 12-hour clock

talking about your daily routine

... and the working day

En France ...

although the 24-hour clock is widely used, you'll also come across the 12-hour clock in informal everyday speech. Unlike in English, the hour comes first, then the minutes: so **cinq heures dix** is *ten past five*, **huit heures et quart** is *quarter past eight*. You use **moins** to talk about minutes to the hour: **cinq heures moins dix** is *ten to five* and **huit heures moins le quart** is *quarter to eight*. Half past is **et demie: neuf heures et demie**.

You can add **du matin, de l'après-midi, du soir** in the morning, in the afternoon, in the evening to clarify any ambiguity: **cinq heures du matin** five o'clock in the morning.

Using the 24-hour clock

1 **1•17** Listen to the key language:

Il y a un vol qui part à ...	There's a flight that leaves at ...
Le premier vol ...	The first flight ...
Le vol suivant ...	The following flight ...
Est-ce qu'il y a un vol avant ...?	Is there a flight before ...?
Mon vol arrive à ...	My flight arrives at ...
à seize heures	at 4pm/16.00
quinze/trente/quarante-cinq	15/30/45

2 **1•18** En route from Lima to Bordeaux, Gustavo Fernández misses his connection in Charles de Gaulle airport in Paris. Listen to the information he's given and note what time the next three flights leave, even though the first is full – **complet**.

3 **1•19** Gustavo is in France for **un colloque** *academic conference*. Listen as he rings his contact, Florent Hubert, **professeur à l'université de Bordeaux**, and leaves a message. What time does he say his flight will be arriving?

4 **1•20** At the last minute, the airline got Gustavo on the earlier flight. How will he let Florent know he arrives at 5.20pm, having first apologised for the change in arrangements? Listen to check your answer.

Florent, excusez-moi pour ce changement, mais ....
à .... **heures** ....

... and the 12-hour clock

5 1•21 Listen to the key language:

vers neuf heures moins le quart	about quarter to nine
après ça	after that
entre onze heures et midi	between eleven o'clock and midday
jusqu'à trois heures	until three o'clock

Nous is often used to say *we* in more formal contexts, such as at work. In the present tense, most verbs used with **nous** end in **-ons**:

nous écoutons *we listen* **nous allons** *we go* **nous avons** *we have*

... but **nous sommes** *we are* (from être, *to be*).

G13

6 1•22 Florent tells Gustavo what to expect on the first day of the conference. He begins with **si cela vous convient** *if that's OK with you*.

  a Listen and jot down the seven different times he mentions.

  b Read what he says and fill the gaps with the correct form of the verbs below, in this order. Listen again to check.

partir	arriver	commencer	écouter	aller	parler	inviter

Bon, Gustavo. Demain, si cela vous convient, nous .... de la maison vers neuf heures moins le quart. Nous .... à l'université vers neuf heures et quart. Le colloque .... à dix heures: nous .... un discours du Ministre de l'Écologie. Après ça, entre onze heures et midi, il y a des présentations: nous avons le choix entre plusieurs sujets. À midi, nous .... au restaurant, c'est l'heure de déjeuner. Nous sommes libres jusqu'à trois heures. L'après-midi, nous .... de nos recherches. Le colloque finit avant six heures du soir, mais les organisateurs .... tous les délégués à une dégustation à l'École du Vin.

LE RÉCHAUFFEMENT CLIMATIQUE
● Les causes et les conséquences
COLLOQUE Université de Bordeaux 25–27 avril

Talking about your daily routine

1 1•23 Listen to the key language:

généralement	usually
je me réveille	I wake up
je me lève (tôt/tard)	I get up (early/late)
je rentre chez moi	I go home
je me repose	I relax
je me couche	I go to bed

2 1•24 As you listen to six people talking about their morning routine, jot down whether they wake up or get up at the times listed.

a **7.55** c **8.00** e **8.50**

b **7.30** d **6.45** f **6.30**

En français

The infinitive of some verbs has two parts, the first being **se** (or **s'** before a vowel): **se lever** to get up, **s'appeler** to be called, **se reposer** to relax. These are called reflexive verbs.

The **se** changes to **me, te, se, nous** or **vous**, depending on who is involved:

je me lève I get up	**nous nous levons** we get up
tu te lèves you get up	**vous vous levez** you get up
il/elle se lève he/she gets up	**ils/elles se lèvent** they get up
on se lève we get up	

(Note the spelling change in **lever**: **se lever** but **je me lève**.) **G25**

---

3 1•25 Listen to Florent telling Gustavo about his daily routine (**chaque** means each/every). See if you can catch:

- what time he normally gets up,
- when he does his research,
- what he does in the evening,
- what time he has dinner (**en famille** with his family);
- what time he goes to bed.

4 Now say what time you normally wake up and get up.

... and the working day

5 **1•26** Listen to the key language:

À quelle heure ...?	What time ...?
Il/Elle part de la maison.	He/She leaves the house.
Il/Elle prend le train/la voiture.	He/She takes the train/the car.
Je vais, Il/Elle va à la salle de gym.	I go, He/She goes to the gym.
Je fais, Il/Elle fait du sport.	I do, He/She does sport.

6 **1•27** Listen as Florent's wife Nathalie talks about their routine. Tick the statements that apply to Florent, Nathalie or both of them.

		F	N				F	N
a	Je me réveille tôt.				f	Je pars de la maison à 7h25.		
b	Je me lève à 6h45.				g	Je prends la voiture.		
c	Je me lève à 8h.				h	Je fais du sport.		
d	Je travaille à la maison.				i	Je vais à la piscine.		
e	Je suis webdesigner.				j	Je dîne vers 7h.		

Some key verbs don't follow the regular patterns, including these:

aller *to go*	je vais, il/elle va, vous allez
avoir *to have*	j'ai, il/elle a, vous avez
être *to be*	je suis, il/elle est, vous êtes
faire *to do, to make*	je fais, il/elle fait, vous faites
prendre *to take*	je prends, il/elle prend, vous prenez

These irregular verbs have to be learned individually. **G14**

En français

---

7 How would Nathalie ask you (**vous**) these questions?

   a Do you get up early?

   b Do you work at home?

   c Do you do sport every day (**tous les jours**)?

8 Can you say what time someone you know wakes up/gets up and ask someone questions about their daily routine?

put it all together

1 Find a connection between the words in the two columns.

a le vol	1 le colloque
b la dégustation	2 le matin
c les recherches	3 l'École du Vin
d se réveiller	4 l'aéroport
e le discours	5 l'université

2 Write the following in French, in 12-hour clock format.

a at **07.30** à sept heures et demie du matin

b at **20.00** ....

c at **16.15** ....

d at **06.20** ....

e at **23.00** ....

3 Fill each gap with the right form of the verb in brackets.

a **Sylvie est architecte. Elle .... à Rouen.** (travailler)
b **Le colloque .... à neuf heures et demie.** (commencer)
c **Il y a un vol qui .... à huit heures cinq.** (partir)
d **Mon mari et moi, on .... à la maison.** (travailler)
e **Nous .... du programme de demain.** (parler)
f **Le week-end, je .... à neuf heures.** (se lever)
g **Vous .... à quelle heure le matin?** (sortir)
h **Mes enfants .... très tôt.** (se lever)

4 How would you tell someone in French that you:

- usually wake up early;
- get up at 7.30am;
- take the train;
- relax in the evening;
- go to bed at 11pm?

1   **1•28** Answer these questions as if you were Steve Corcoran from the south-east of England.

- **Steve, vous habitez où?**
- ◆ Say you live in Guildford.
- **Mais vous travaillez à Londres, n'est-ce pas?**
- ◆ Say yes, you take the train.
- **Vous vous levez généralement à quelle heure?**
- ◆ Say you usually wake up at half past six and get up at ten to seven.
- **Et vous partez de la maison à quelle heure?**
- ◆ Say at half past seven.
- **Vous rentrez tard le soir?**
- ◆ Say yes, you come home at quarter to eight.

2   **1•29** Now answer the questions as if you were Steve's wife, Bryony.

- **Bryony, Steve se lève à quelle heure?**
- ◆ Say he gets up at ten past seven.
- **Il travaille où?**
- ◆ Say he works in London and leaves the house at half past seven.
- **Et vous, vous travaillez aussi?**
- ◆ Say yes, you work from nine until two in the afternoon.
- **Vous aimez faire du sport?**
- ◆ Say yes, you go to the gym every day.
- **Le soir, vous dînez ensemble?** (**Ensemble** *together.*)
- ◆ Say yes, you have dinner together at home.
- **Vous dînez à quelle heure?**
- ◆ Say you usually have dinner at eight in the evening.

quiz

1 What time is **quatre heures moins vingt-cinq de l'après-midi**? And how would you say it using the 24-hour clock?

2 Is **tard** or **tôt** the French for *early*?

3 What is **le réchauffement climatique**?

4 Add **quarante** and **douze**. What's the answer in French?

5 Is it **me**, **te** or **se** that's missing here? **Elle ...... réveille à sept heures.**

6 Which of these is the odd one out: **tous les jours, le soir, les recherches, le week-end**?

7 What's the connection between **vais** and **allons**?

8 Are you more likely to use **se coucher** in the morning or the evening?

Now check whether you can ...

- understand and say times using both the 12- and 24-hour clock
- say what happens when
- talk about your daily routine
- describe your and another person's work routine

This first section of *Talk French 2* has been about revisiting the basics as well as extending your French. There's more practice in **En plus** but, if you're finding at this stage that some of what you learnt previously has escaped your memory, now would be a good time to remind yourself of numbers (see page 131), vocabulary and key basics. It can be quite therapeutic to go over something familiar that you learnt very early on.

En plus 1

When talking about going **to** or being **in** a place, you use:

- **à** with towns and cities: **à Strasbourg**, **à Leeds**.
- **en** with countries and regions that are feminine (the majority): **en Espagne**, **en Grande-Bretagne**, **en Provence**.
- **au** with countries that are masculine and singular: **au Japon**, **au Canada**, **au Mali**, **au Portugal**, **au Luxembourg**, **au Pays de Galles** *Wales*, **au Royaume-Uni** *UK*.
- **aux** with plural countries: **aux États-Unis** *USA*, **aux Pays-Bas** *Netherlands*.

G3

1   Following the word order of these examples, make up 12 new sentences, each mentioning a different person/people and a different country.

Mon fils	travaille	à	Nantes.
Ils	habitent	en	Finlande.
Je	vais	au	Japon.
Vous	allez	aux	États-Unis.
Nom	va	en	Bretagne.

2   How quickly can you unscramble these member states of the **Union Européenne (l'UE)**? How would you say you're going to these countries?

a   RUM OX BULGE
b   POLAR TUG
c   FINAL END
d   A BYPASS
e   SAGE PEN
f   AN IDLER

Here's the French for four more member states. What are they called in English?

g   la Lettonie
h   l'Autriche
i   la Pologne
j   la Suède

There are different ways of forming feminine job titles:

- add -e:
  il est employé de bureau/elle est employée de banque
- -ier becomes -ière:
  il est infirmier/elle est infirmière
- -ien becomes -ienne:
  musicien/musicienne, pharmacien/pharmacienne
- -eur becomes -euse or -rice:
  chanteur/chanteuse, vendeur/vendeuse
  acteur/actrice, directeur/directrice
- For many jobs, the same word applies to a man or woman:
  il/elle est professeur, comptable, journaliste, médecin, ingénieur.

4 By coincidence, these students on a language course in France discover they all work in the entertainment business. Can you introduce each person, giving their name, home town and country, their job and how long they've been doing it? The first one is done for you.

a Je vous présente Uwe: il habite à Constance, en Allemagne. Il est employé au guichet de location d'un théâtre depuis quatre ans.

Box office employees:
a Uwe, Constance, Germany, four years in his job
b Yuki, Kobe, Japan, 13 years in her job

c Chuck, New York, USA, actor since 2003
d Rita, Toronto, Canada, actress for six months

e Emily, Bradford, UK, singer since 2005

f Vladimir, Moscow, Russia, a musician for 20 years

To ask a question, you can:

- raise your voice towards the end of a statement:
  Vous travaillez à Bordeaux?
- begin with **Est-ce-que: Est-ce que vous travaillez à Bordeaux?**
- invert the subject and verb: **Travaillez-vous à Bordeaux?**

To use a question word (**pourquoi, quand, comment, où**) you can:

- tag it on to the end of a statement: **Vous travaillez où?**
- put it first, with **est-ce que** next: **Où est-ce que vous travaillez?**
- put it first and invert the subject and verb: **Où travaillez-vous?**

4 Read Gustavo's conversation with a delegate at the global warming conference. Find out what kind of work he does and what she suggests they do in the evening. Then list in English nine questions they ask.

- **Est-ce que cette place est libre?**
- ◆ **Oui, bien sûr ... bonjour, je m'appelle Gustavo Fernández.**
- **Enchantée, je m'appelle Christine Nicot. Vous êtes d'où?**
- ◆ **Je suis du Pérou. Et vous, êtes-vous française?**
- **Oui, mais j'habite en Bretagne, pas ici à Bordeaux. Heureusement!**
- ◆ **Pourquoi dites-vous* ça?**
- **Je n'aime pas du tout les grandes villes; je préfère mon village, près de la mer!**
- ◆ **Ah bon! Qu'est-ce que vous faites comme travail?**
- **Je travaille pour une association de protection de l'environnement sous-marin. Ça me passionne! Et vous, vous travaillez où?**
- ◆ **Je suis étudiant, je fais des recherches sur les changements climatiques dans les zones désertiques. On est à l'opposé: vous, l'eau, moi, le désert!**
- **Oui! Le colloque finit à quelle heure ce soir? Je voudrais me promener* au bord* de la Garonne – vous voulez venir avec moi?**
- ◆ **Oui, mais vous n'allez pas à la dégustation de vin avec les autres délégués?**
- **Bof!**

* **vous dites** *you say*; **me promener** *go for a walk*;
  au bord *on the riverbank/along the riverside*; **Bof!** *I'd rather not.*

A large number of verbs end in -er, all of them regular except **aller** *to go*. Some verbs which end in -ir and -re follow regular patterns.

● Regular -ir verbs include **finir** *to finish* and **choisir** *to choose*:

je finis	nous finissons
tu finis	vous finissez
il/elle/on finit	ils/elles finissent

● Regular -re verbs include **attendre** *to wait* and **vendre** *to sell*:

j'attends	nous attendons
tu attends	vous attendez
il/elle/on attend	ils/elles attendent

G13

5 Océane is working at a holiday camp during the summer. She writes to her friend Thierry about her job organising activities for children. Complete the verbs with the right endings.

> Salut, Thierry!
> Ça va? Je travaill…… sur la Côte d'Azur, je suis animatrice dans une colonie de vacances. J'aim…… beaucoup travailler avec les enfants. J'habit…… dans un chalet avec deux Espagnoles: elles s'appell…… Marisa et Gina. Nous parl…… espagnol ensemble. C'est super.
> Je me lèv…… tôt chaque matin, à 7 heures, parce que les activités commenc…… à 8h. On fait du sport et on organis…… des jeux sur la plage. Mon travail fin…… à 18h. Après le dîner, je me repos…… un peu, et vers 21h, je sor…… avec mes amies. On aim…… aller au restaurant ou dans un club. On se couch…… vers 2h du matin!
> Et toi, qu'est-ce que tu fais? Tu attend…… les résultats de tes examens? Quand est-ce que tu par…… en vacances?
> À bientôt!
> Bisous, Océane

6 Imagine you're Thierry and reply to Océane's letter. Say that:

● you get up at 10am
● you work from 6pm until 11pm, you're a waiter in a café
● you're leaving for your holiday on the 15th of August (**le 15 août**), you're going to Italy.

Add other details of your own choice if you wish.

Il faut réserver à l'avance?

getting local information

... and advice

talking about leisure interests

arranging an activity

En France ...

looking beyond the better-known beaches and ski resorts, there's plenty of spectacular scenery to discover. Scattered all over France and the **départements d'outre-mer** *overseas departments* such as Guadeloupe, there are nine **parcs nationaux** *national parks*, 45 **parcs naturels régionaux** *regional nature parks* and 320 **réserves naturelles** *nature reserves*. Information is available from **La Maison de la France**, France's official tourist organisation, or from any local **office du tourisme** or **syndicat d'initiative**. You'll discover wonderful countryside and a wide choice of open-air activities all year round, ranging from a **randonnée** *hike* to any of **les sports extrêmes**.

Getting local information

1 1•30 Listen to the key language:

Il y a ... près d'ici?	Is/Are there ... round here?
Est-ce qu'il y a ...?	Is/Are there ...?
Il y en a beaucoup.	There are a lot of them.
(Est-ce que) je peux...	Can I ...?
(Est-ce qu')on peut ...?	Can we ...?
Est-ce que vous savez (si) ...?	Do you know (if) ...?

2 Informations touristiques publications such as the following are freely available in French tourist offices. See if you can work out what these are, using the glossary if necessary.

Guide des restaurants   Plan de la ville   Carte routière

Carte de la région   Carte de la région   Guide des campings

Liste des auberges de jeunesse   Guide des chambres d'hôtes

Calendrier des événements sportifs   Dépliants touristiques

Horaires d'ouverture du musée

3 1•31 Listen to people making enquiries at the **office du tourisme (OT)** and tick the items above as you hear them. Listen out for **gratuit** *free*.

To ask if you can do something, say je peux ...? or on peut ...?, making sure your voice goes up at the end so that it sounds like a question.

Peux and peut are from pouvoir *to be able to*, which is an irregular verb and is followed by an infinitive:

je peux	nous pouvons
tu peux	vous pouvez
il/elle/on peut	ils/elles peuvent

... and advice

4 1•32 Listen to the key language:

Qu'est-ce qu'il y a	What is there
... à faire/voir?	... to do/to see?
Si vous voulez ...	If you want ...
Si vous aimez/préférez ...	If you like/prefer ...
Vous devez (aller visiter ...)	You must (go and visit ...)
Il faut absolument aller le voir.	You really must go and see it.

5 1•33 As you listen to another tourist making enquiries at the **OT**, listen out for the following and tick them as you hear them.

un vélo

une piste cyclable

un vignoble

un château

un lac

une randonnée

To advise people what they must or should do, you use **devoir** *to have to*. It's an irregular verb, followed by an infinitive:

je dois	nous devons
tu dois	vous devez
il/elle/on doit	ils/elles doivent

6 1•33 Now read the conversation you've just heard and fill in the gaps.

- Qu'est-ce qu'il y a à .... dans la région?
- Si vous .... la nature, vous .... absolument faire une randonnée: il y a beaucoup de superbes sentiers pour ça dans les environs. Si vous préférez, vous .... louer un vélo: les pistes cyclables sont très jolies aussi. Si vous .... goûter aux vins de la région, vous .... aller visiter un de nos vignobles: il y en a beaucoup par ici. Aux alentours de la ville, il y a un lac où on .... faire de la voile ou de la planche à voile. Et puis il y a le château, bien sûr – il .... absolument aller le voir.

Talking about leisure interests

1   1•34 Listen to the key language:

Je fais du ski nautique/ **de la planche à voile.**	I go waterskiing/windsurfing.
Tu fais du sport?	Do you do any sport?
J'aime surtout …	I particularly like …
Je n'aime pas tellement …	I don't much like …
Ça me plaît (beaucoup).	I like it (very much).

2   1•35 Listen to Lucas, Chantal and Sophie talking about what they like to do, and note their interests.

l'escalade *climbing*	**le snowboard** *snowboarding*
le ski nautique *waterskiing*	**la planche à voile** *windsurfing*
le taekwondo *taekwondo*	**la randonnée** *hiking*

En français

Whereas in English we often use *go* when talking about sport, e.g. *I go climbing*, French expressions to do with sport use **faire**: je fais de l'escalade.

Faire is followed by **du, de la, de l'** or **des**:

Je fais du ski. (masculine singular)

Elle fait de la planche à voile. (feminine singular)

Vous faites de l'escalade. (singular beginning with a vowel)

Lucas fait des arts martiaux? (plural)

3   1•36 Read this list of phrases, then listen to Sophie's brother talking about going out in the Pyrenees. Tick the phrases you hear. Then listen again to spot **ne … personne** *nobody* and **ne … jamais** *never*: they go around a verb, like **ne … pas** *not*.

☐ **on fait des randonnées**	☐ **j'aime beaucoup la nature**
☐ **on fait du vélo**	☐ **des paysages magnifiques**
☐ **de petits sentiers isolés**	☐ **des aigles**

4   Have a go at talking about your interests – your own (**je fais du/de la/ des …**) and any that you share with others (**on fait du/de la/des …**).

Arranging an activity

1 1•37 Listen to the key language:

Il faut ...	It's necessary to/You need to ...
Il ne faut pas ...	You don't need to ...
Je vous conseille d'apporter ...	I advise you to bring ...
Je voudrais louer ...	I'd like to hire ...
Est-ce qu'il y a un tarif réduit?	Is there a reduction?

> **Il faut** is followed by an infinitive to say what needs to be done.
> It can refer to me, you, someone else or everyone in general.
> **Il faut réserver.** *You need to book.*
>
> **G15**

2 1•38 Listen to a visitor asking about guided walks, and note which of the points below is NOT mentioned. Then read the transcript on page 112.

- You don't need to book.
- There's a walk every day.
- They start at 10.00.
- They last about three and a half hours.
- Sun cream and a sunhat are recommended.
- You need to take warm clothing.
- It's important to wear suitable shoes.
- You need to bring a flask of water.

3 1•39 Listen and read as Thierry tells Nicole about a day out he's going to have with a friend tomorrow. What is he thinking of doing? **Y** means *there*, and goes before the verb.

T **Demain, on va à la réserve naturelle pour explorer un peu.**
N **Vous y allez comment? À pied ou en voiture? Je te conseille de louer des scooters. Ce n'est pas très cher.**
T **Y aller en scooter? Géniale comme idée!**

4 1•40 Thierry's friend isn't keen on a **scooter** so they decide to hire mountain bikes (**vélos tout terrain – VTTs**). Listen as Thierry rings the hire company and note:

- how long they want the bikes for;
- how much it costs per bike;
- how much discount is offered.

put it all together

1 Fill the gap with the correct form – **du**, **de la**, **de l'** or **des**.

   a Vous aimez faire .... escalade?
   b Tu fais .... sport?
   c En été, je fais .... planche à voile.
   d Mon frère aime faire .... arts martiaux.
   e On peut faire .... ski nautique sur le lac.

2 Match the two halves of sentences.

a	Je préfère	1	au château.
b	On peut faire	2	réserver
c	Je vous conseille	3	du vélo.
d	Vous devez aller	4	à visiter?
e	Qu'est-ce qu'il y a	5	le ski.
f	Il faut	6	comment?
g	Vous y allez	7	de louer des scooters.

3 Your teenage neighbour has received an e-mail from a friend she met in France and can't read all of it. Explain to her what this extract says, using the glossary for any new words.

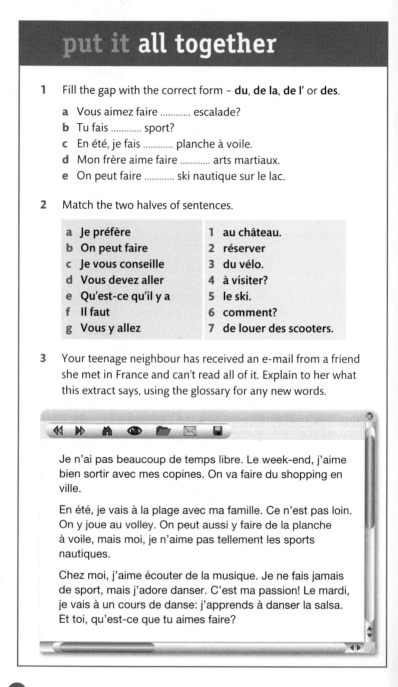

Je n'ai pas beaucoup de temps libre. Le week-end, j'aime bien sortir avec mes copines. On va faire du shopping en ville.

En été, je vais à la plage avec ma famille. Ce n'est pas loin. On y joue au volley. On peut aussi y faire de la planche à voile, mais moi, je n'aime pas tellement les sports nautiques.

Chez moi, j'aime écouter de la musique. Je ne fais jamais de sport, mais j'adore danser. C'est ma passion! Le mardi, je vais à un cours de danse: j'apprends à danser la salsa. Et toi, qu'est-ce que tu aimes faire?

1   1•41 Imagine you're at the tourist office in Roussillon.

- **Bonjour. Je peux vous aider?**
- ◆ Greet her and ask if they have a map of the area.
- **Oui, voilà. Et voici une carte routière aussi.**
- ◆ Ask what there is to do in the area.
- **Eh bien, il y a beaucoup d'endroits très jolis à visiter. Et le parc du Luberon est tout près. Vous aimez la nature?**
- ◆ Say yes, you'd like to go on a hike in the park.
- **Eh bien, oui, c'est possible. Il y a des visites guidées à pied ou à vélo. Voici des renseignements. Les visites sont très populaires: il faut réserver à l'avance.**
- ◆ Ask if you (**on**) can hire scooters.
- **Pas à Roussillon, mais on peut louer des scooters ou des vélos à Gordes.**
- ◆ Thank her and ask if there's a good restaurant in Roussillon.
- **Oui, si vous aimez la cuisine provençale, je vous conseille le restaurant Le Jardin, juste en face de l'Office du Tourisme.**

2   1•42 You're chatting to Hugo, who you've met on holiday.

- Ask him what he does at the weekend. (Use **tu**.)
- ◆ **Je vais en ville, je fais un peu de shopping, et le samedi soir, je sors avec mes amis. On va au cinéma.**
- Ask him if he does any sport.
- ◆ **Oui, je fais du vélo et j'aime bien nager aussi.**
- Ask him if he likes football.
- ◆ **J'adore regarder le foot à la télé. Je suis supporter de l'Olympique de Marseille. Et toi, qu'est-ce tu aimes faire pendant ton temps libre?**

3   Using the information above, tell an English friend what Hugo does at the weekend. Then practise replying to the question: **Qu'est-ce tu aimes faire pendant ton temps libre?** *What do you like to do in your spare time?*

quiz

1 What is **une carte routière**?

2 Would you use **peux** or **peut** with **on**?

3 Which sport is the odd one out: **le ski nautique**, **l'escalade**, **la planche à voile**, **nager**?

4 Can you think of another way of saying **Vous devez réserver à l'avance**?

5 What does **y** mean?

6 If you were travelling on **une piste cyclable**, would you be on a **vélo** or in a **voiture**?

7 Which verb goes before **du snowboard**, **du bowling**, **des randonnées**, **de la planche à voile**?

8 What's *to hire* in French?

Now check whether you can ...

- ask for information and advice in a tourist office
- ask whether you can do something
- arrange an activity
- talk about what you like to do in your spare time
- ask others about their leisure interests

If you access **www.fr.franceguide.com**, the official website of La Maison de la France, you can read plenty of fascinating and useful information about France as well as competitions and offers. Try to 'skim', i.e. don't get hung up on single words that you don't understand, but try to get the flow of the passage. There's an English version of the site which you can use to compare the information given in each language.

Quelle belle maison!

reading property descriptions

describing a property

enquiring about a gîte to rent

showing someone round a house

En France ...

lots of visitors choose to **louer** *rent* or to **faire un échange de maisons** *do a house swap*, rather than stay in a hotel. More and more people are buying property in France, attracted by **une villa de luxe**, **un chalet** in the mountains, **un appartement** in a beach resort, or possibly **une ancienne ferme restaurée**, an old farmhouse which has been restored. What motivates them? Is it **le climat**, **la culture**, **la gastronomie**, **la mode**, or simply the quality of life, **la qualité de la vie**?

Reading property descriptions

À VENDRE ...

EXCEPTIONNEL Superbe villa à proximité de la mer.
5 chambres, 2 sdb, cuisine, salon/salle à manger, salle de billard.
Piscine chauffée. Garage indépendant (4 voitures). Écurie.
985 000€.

AU CALME, à 30 km de Lyon, joli village. Ancienne ferme
restaurée, sur 2 niveaux. Cuisine équipée, séjour, 4 chambres,
2 wc, sdb avec baignoire et douche. Dépendances. Jardin.
Chauffage électrique.

À VOIR ET À SAISIR Chalet, très calme, tout confort, rénové avec
goût, cheminée. 2 chambres. Jardin arboré, barbecue.
175 000€.

MAISON de charme dans un village, à côté d'un lac, en
partie restaurée avec beaucoup de soin et de confort. Séjour,
bureau, 4 chambres, dressing, 2 sdb. Terrasse avec barbecue.
Investissement idéal.

APPARTEMENT 2 chambres, cuisine équipée sur séjour, placard
dans chambres. État neuf. **Prix à discuter.**

1 Look at the property profiles from the **agence immobilière** *estate
agent's* and see how many of the words you know or can guess. Then
work through the profiles systematically, consulting the glossary where
you need to, and list the words for:

a five types of house;
b at least nine different rooms;
c at least four outside features.

Describing a property

1 **1•43** Listen to the key language:

Il/Elle est comment?	What's it like?
Tu peux/Vous pouvez me décrire ...	Can you describe (for me) ...
... ta/votre maison?	... your house?
... ton/votre appartement?	... your flat?
Il/Elle se trouve ...	It's (located) ...
C'est une maison qui est ...	It's a house that is ...

2 **1•44** Listen as a) a retired couple, b) a woman living on her own, and c) a young man living with friends are asked about where they live. Jot down a, b or c by the words that describe their homes.

jolie	une belle terrasse	le balcon
ancienne	pratique	restaurée
vieille	toutes les facilités à proximité	un beau jardin
neuf	à l'extérieur de la ville	calme
	au centre-ville	

3 **1•45** The couple go on to describe their house in detail. Listen and say:

- how many bedrooms it has,
- how many bathrooms,
- where they eat,
- which room has the French window (**une porte-fenêtre**, literally *door-window*),
- what's special about the terrace.

Listen for the fruit trees at the end: what two fruits would they yield?

Enquiring about a gîte to rent

1   Laura Wilson finds an advert for a **gîte**, available **à louer** *to rent*.

LA MIRABELLE

Gîte à la campagne, à 3km de la mer, avec 3 chambres, salon, cuisine, 1 sdb, 1 wc. Terrasse couverte, grand jardin. 460–820€/sem. 110–130€/nuit.

Électro-ménager ▪ Machine à laver ▪ Lave-vaisselle ▪ Four ▪ Réfrigérateur ▪ Congélateur ▪ Micro-ondes ▪ Chauffage

Multimédia ▪ TV ▪ Téléphone ▪ DVD

Aménagements ▪Terrasse ▪ Jardin ▪ BBQ ▪ Terrain de boules ▪ Emplacement pour garer la voiture

Services ▪ Ménage ▪ Draps

Environs ▪ Équitation ▪ Golf ▪ Sports nautiques ▪ Tennis ▪ Pêche ▪ Piscine

How would Laura tell her English partner:

a   how far it is from the sea,

b   the number of bedrooms/bathrooms,

c   how much it will cost for a week,

d   if there's anywhere to park,

e   if sheets are provided,

f   what there is to do locally?

2   1●46 Listen to the key language:

Allô.	Hello. (*on the phone*)
Le gîte est disponible.	The gîte is available.
Il y a combien de ...?	How many ... are there?
Il y en a quatre.	There are four (<u>of them</u>).
Il n'y a pas de garage/ serviettes.	There isn't a garage./There aren't any towels.
À quel étage?	On which floor?

3   1●47 Listen to Laura's conversation with the owner of another villa and say whether these are true or false.   **vrai**   **faux**

a   Le gîte est disponible à partir du 22 avril.

b   Il n'y a pas de draps.

c   Il y a trois salles de bains.

d   Il y a un garage.

e   Il y a une machine à laver.

Showing someone round a house

1 **1•48** Listen to the key language:

Quelle belle maison!	What a beautiful house!
C'est quelle clé?	Which key is it?
C'est (si) joli!	It's (so) pretty!
Il/Elle est très/plutôt ...	It's very/rather ...
Il/Elle est assez ...	It's quite ...
Bon séjour!	Enjoy your stay!

> **Quel** (m) and **quelle** (f) have two meanings:
>
> • *what* or *which* + noun, in a question: **Elles sont à quel étage?**
> *Which floor are they on?* **C'est quelle chambre?** *Which bedroom is it?*
>
> • *What a ...* in an exclamation: **Quel beau jardin!** *What a
> beautiful garden!* **Quelle belle vue!** *What a beautiful view!* **G30**

2 **1•49** Laura decides on La Mirabelle. Listen as the owner shows her round, and fill the gaps with **quel**, **quelle**, **assez**, **plutôt**, **si** or **très**.

- ● Entrez, entrez. Voici le séjour: il est .... grand, et vous avez la porte-fenêtre qui donne sur la terrasse.
- ◆ .... beau jardin! C'est .... clé pour ouvrir la porte-fenêtre?
- ● C'est la .... petite clé-là, madame.
- ◆ Merci.
- ● Voici la cuisine. Vous avez le frigo, le congélateur, la machine à laver, le lave-vaisselle, le micro-ondes, le four ...
- ◆ Ah oui, elle est .... bien équipée et .... grande.
- ● Au premier étage, il y a les chambres. La troisième est .... petite, mais la vue de la fenêtre est superbe.
- ◆ C'est .... joli ici! .... belle maison!
- ● Alors, voilà. Bon séjour!

3 **1•50** Listening out for the key words **cent** *hundred(s)* and **mille** *thousand(s)*, write down how much these properties cost.

- **a** maison jumelée *semi-detached* avec garage ......
- **b** appartement tout neuf ......
- **c** maison totalement restaurée ......
- **d** villa, six pièces ......
- **e** gîte avec piscine ......

put it all together

1   From this list of words and phrases, find six pairs of opposites (e.g. **grand/petit**). You're left with one word – what is it?

jumelé	loin	montagne	neuf
équipé	petit	ancien	près
séparé	grand	en banlieue	mer
	en plein centre-ville		

2   What's the French for the areas labelled a-h?

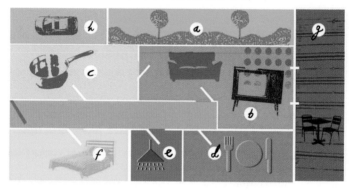

3   Write in French a profile of these two properties, of the kind used to advertise places for sale or rent.

> À VENDRE Flat, brand new, with sea view, 5 minutes from the beach. Balcony. 2 bedrooms, 2 bathrooms.

> À LOUER Renovated gîte, peaceful, all facilities nearby. Very pretty. Sitting room, well-equipped kitchen, study, 4 bedrooms, 3 bathrooms. Large garden and terrace.

4   Now try writing a similar short description of your own home.

1   1•51 You've got the phone number of a French holiday house called Le Rossignol, and call for more information.

- ● **Le Rossignol. Allô.**
- ◆ Say you'd like to rent a gîte in Provence. Ask if he'll describe Le Rossignol for you.
- ● **Oui, bien sûr. C'est un joli gîte avec terrasse et jardin.**
- ◆ Ask if it's near the sea.
- ● **Il se trouve à quatre kilomètres environ d'une très belle plage.**
- ◆ Ask how many bedrooms there are.
- ● **Il y en a trois. Le gîte est pour sept personnes maximum.**
- ◆ And how many bathrooms are there?
- ● **Il y en a une, au premier étage.**
- ◆ Hmm, that's not enough for your family. Ask if there's a washing machine.
- ● **Oui, bien sûr.**
- ◆ You don't want to be washing up on your holiday. Is there a dishwasher?
- ● **Non, monsieur, la cuisine est très petite. Elle date de 1894.**
- ◆ You've heard enough! Say thank you and goodbye.

2   1•52 You decided against Le Rossignol. Instead, you are now staying in the country near Cavalaire with your family. Someone you meet asks what the house is like.

- ● **Il est comment, votre gîte?**
- ◆ Say it's a restored farmhouse.
- ● **Elle se trouve où?**
- ◆ Say it's five kilometres from Cavalaire.
- ● **Elle est grande, la ferme? Il y a combien de chambres?**
- ◆ Say there are five of them.
- ● **Ah oui, elle est grande alors!**
- ◆ Say yes, and the kitchen is very big and very well equipped.
- ● **C'est super! Vous avez un jardin?**
- ◆ Say there's a small garden and a beautiful terrace.
- ● **Très bien, alors, bon séjour!**

quiz

1 Give two meanings of **séjour**.
2 If a property is **en partie restaurée**, what state is it in?
3 Would you use **vieux** or **vieille** to describe **une ferme**?
4 Do you wash clothes in a **machine à laver** or a **lave-vaisselle**?
5 Apart from *nine* what else does **neuf** mean?
6 How would you say *What a beautiful beach*?
7 To say *It's rather small* what word do you need in the gap here? **C'est** .... **petit**.
8 If a gîte is available from 3rd May, would it be **disponible à partir du 3 mai** or **disponible avant le 3 mai**?

Now check whether you can ...

- understand the key words in property descriptions
- make enquiries about renting a gîte
- describe your own home
- show someone round your house
- comment on a house and compliment its owner
- understand prices in hundreds and thousands of euros

Memory training techniques can be used to good effect when learning a language. Start with a simple sentence such as **Je voudrais un gîte en France** then add to it in small increments: **Je voudrais un gîte en France avec piscine**, adding more as you mentally zoom in: **Je voudrais un très beau gîte en France avec piscine, quatre chambres et lave-vaisselle** – until you're describing your ideal property in detail and creating a substantial sentence in French.

En plus 2

1 France's 22 **régions** each have their own distinct character. Read the descriptions of three of them, work out which they are and find them on the map.

a **L'Alsace** est la plus petite région de la France après la Corse. Elle est située dans le nord-est du pays à côté de la frontière allemande. Les habitants de cette région ont une forte identité culturelle, à la fois française et germanique. La ville la plus importante de la région est Strasbourg.

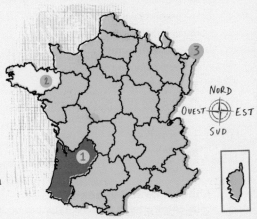

b Cette région est connue pour ses vins de qualité et sa gastronomie. **L'Aquitaine** se trouve dans le sud-ouest de la France à côté de la frontière espagnole. Bordeaux est la capitale régionale. En été, il y a beaucoup de fêtes gastronomiques, culturelles et littéraires.

c Les paysages de **la Bretagne** sont très différents: à l'intérieur, la campagne est belle et il y a des forêts magnifiques. Sur la côte, on trouve de belles plages de sable et de petits ports très pittoresques.

Plural nouns need plural adjectives, masculine or feminine. Most adjectives add -e and -s: **grand** (m), **grands** (mpl), **grande** (f), **grandes** (fpl). If the masculine form ends in -e, then m and f are identical: **pittoresque** (m or f), **pittoresques** (mpl or fpl).

Irregular: **beau** (m), **beaux** (mpl), **belle** (f), **belles** (fpl).

When a plural adjective is placed before a noun, it follows **de**, not **des**: compare **de belles plages** with **des forêts magnifiques**. **G4**

En français

2 Ronan and Eleanor O'Connor are planning a walking holiday with another couple and are looking for a gîte near **lac Léman** *Lake Geneva.* They know what they want and they're searching websites. Read the details of two properties below and put a ✓ or ✗ against each item in the list to show whether they meet the criteria.

		1	2
a	near the lake		
b	nice view		
c	property with a bit of character		
d	sleeps four comfortably		
e	two bathrooms		
f	well-equipped kitchen		
g	quiet location		
h	shops nearby		
i	somewhere to eat outside		
j	car parking		
k	heating		

1

À louer: La Soleillade

Gîte entièrement rénové avec beaucoup de charme dans un village tranquille, à 20km du lac Léman. Idéal pour les amoureux de la nature. Boulangerie et bureau de poste au village.
2 chambres, 1 salle de bains, 1 WC. Cuisine bien équipée, salon. Chauffage central. 1 lit simple, 2 lits doubles, 1 lit d'enfant.
Jardin: 650m² avec terrasse. Parking privé.
Orientation: sud. Vue: campagne.

2

À louer: Les Abris

Gîte neuf 1–4 personnes.
Maison de charme sur jardin clos. Supermarché, casino, cinéma à 400m. À 0,5km des sports, ski nautique, voile, sur lac Léman.
3 pièces: 1 chambre, salle à manger, coin-cuisine, salon avec canapé-lit, 1 salle d'eau, 1 WC indépendant.
Terrasse, véranda, jardin (100m²), salon de jardin, barbecue, parking privé. Date de construction: 2004.
Animaux acceptés. Vue: lac.

3 The O'Connors have settled on **La Soleillade** and write an e-mail to the **propriétaire** *owner*, asking for more information. See if you can read the email without using the glossary, then check the English translation on page 115.

Cher Monsieur

Je voudrais savoir si votre gîte est disponible la première semaine de septembre (du 1er au 8 septembre). Nous sommes quatre personnes: mon mari et moi-même et un autre couple. Pourriez-vous me dire combien il coûte et si on doit payer des arrhes? Je voudrais aussi savoir s'il y a une machine à laver et un congélateur dans la cuisine.

Je vous remercie d'avance.

Meilleurs sentiments,

Eleanor O'Connor

4 Using Eleanor's e-mail as your model, write an e-mail to M. Bourdon, saying:

- you'd like to know if La Soleillade is available for two weeks, from 18 August to 1 September, for three friends and you;
- could he tell you the price for two weeks and whether he takes a deposit;
- you'd like to know whether there's a dishwasher and a microwave.

5 In his reply, M. Bourdon lists the kitchen equipment. Read it, check any new words in the glossary, then close the book and have a go at saying what's in your own kitchen, starting with **Dans ma cuisine, il y a ...**

La cuisine est très bien équipée: il y a un réfrigérateur, un congélateur, un four, des plaques de cuisson, un micro-ondes, un lave-vaisselle, une machine à laver, un aspirateur, un fer à repasser et une bouilloire électrique.

Words expressing possession have plural forms for use with plural nouns:

Où sont <u>mes</u> lunettes? *Where are my glasses?*

Ce sont <u>tes</u> gants? *Are these your gloves?*

The plural of **mon/ma** is **mes**, of **ton/ta** is **tes**, and of **son/sa** is **ses**.

The plurals of **notre** and **votre** are **nos** and **vos**.   **G6**

6 The O'Connors and their friends, Debbie and Matt, are now packing for their holiday. Eleanor is getting in the mood and checking items on her list in French. What word is needed to complete each sentence?

a Où sont (my) .... **lunettes de soleil?**

b Matt, c'est (your) .... **sac à dos, ça?**

c Et ce sont (his) .... **chaussures de marche, je crois.**

d Ronan, tu as (your) .... **lampe?**

e Tu cherches (my) .... **crème solaire, s'il te plaît, Ronan?**

f Debbie, n'oublie pas (your) .... **appareil-photo!**

Some items are owned jointly:

g Matt et Debbie, c'est (your) .... **boussole?**

h Ah, je ne trouve pas (our) .... **jumelles.**

 la lampe

 les chaussures de marche

 le sac à dos

 l'appareil-photo

 la crème solaire

 les lunettes de soleil

 la boussole

 les jumelles

À mon avis ...

shopping for clothes

... and shoes and bags

expressing your opinion

... and making comparisons

En France ...

fashion, **la mode**, is considered an art form as well as one of the country's biggest exports – think of legendary **créateurs** *designers* such as Christian Dior, Yves Saint Laurent, Jean-Paul Gaultier, Sonya Rykiel, Azzedine Alaïa ... Many English words to do with clothes and fashion are taken from French – chic, boutique, décolleté, lingerie, camisole, prêt-à-porter. French has adopted some of our fashion vocabulary too: **un polo, un tee-shirt, un blazer, un cardigan, un pull** *pullover*. Not everything is a straightforward translation: **une veste** is a jacket, **des baskets** are trainers and **un smoking** is a dinner jacket. **Un jean** is a pair of jeans but **en jean** describes any garment made from denim: **une jupe en jean** *denim skirt*. The word denim itself comes from **(serge) de Nîmes**, named after a type of cloth from that southern French town.

Shopping for clothes

1 1•53 Listen to the key language.

Je cherche ...	I'm looking for ...
... un pantalon blanc	... a pair of white trousers
... une chemise blanche	... a white shirt
... un pull en laine	... a woollen jumper
ce tee-shirt, cette veste	this T-shirt (m), this jacket (f)
taille quarante	size 40
Il/Elle coûte combien?	How much is it?

2 1•54 First, read the words in the box. Then listen to some conversations in clothes shops and jot down in English what people are looking for.

noir(e) black	**blanc(he)** white	**gris(e)** grey	**vert(e)** green
rouge red	**jaune** yellow	**bleu(e)** blue	

lin linen	**pure laine** pure wool	**pur coton** pure cotton
soie silk	**cachemire** cashmere	

	vêtement garment	**couleur** colour	**matière** fabric	**taille** size
a				
b				
c				
d				
e				
f				

To say *this* or *that*, use **ce** (m sing) or **cet** (before a vowel), **cette** (f sing) and **ces** (pl):

ce pull *this/that pullover*	**cet appareil-photo** *this camera*
cette veste *this/that jacket*	**ces bottes** *these/those boots* **G7**

3 1•55 Listen to a couple out shopping, then answer the questions:

a What are they looking for?   **c** Who is it for?

b What two colours do they ask for?   **d** How much does it cost?

... and shoes and bags

4 1•56 Listen to the key language.

Je voudrais essayer	I'd like to try on
... ces bottes	... these boots
Vous faites quelle pointure?	What size do you take?
Vous voulez les essayer?	Would you like to try them on?
Je n'ai plus de ...	I haven't any more ...
Je n'ai que ...	I've only got ....
Je voudrais l'échanger.	I want to change it.

5 1•57 In a shoe shop, a customer has seen some boots she likes and wants to try them on. Listen and jot down:

- what size she takes
- the sizes of the boots they have in stock
- what different colour she's offered

> The object pronouns **le/la** *it* and **les** *them* usually come before the relevant verb:
>
> **Le cachemire? Je le lave à la main.** *Cashmere? I wash it by hand.*
> **Ma veste rouge? Je la porte souvent.** *My red jacket? I often wear it.*
> **Je voudrais les acheter.** *I'd like to buy them.*
>
> **G32**

6 Using the glossary, read this advert for **un sac à dos** *a backpack*.

a Which word means *waterproof*?

b Is it washable?

c What's the French for *a zip, zipped* and *pocket*?

> Sac à dos ultra léger
> Excellente qualité, imperméable, lavable. Un compartiment principal à fermeture éclair, une poche zippée à l'avant et une poche intérieure zippée. Emplacement téléphone. Idéal pour la randonnée.

7 1•58 A customer returns a backpack because something's **cassé** *broken*. He starts **Il y a un problème avec ce sac à dos** *There's a problem with this backpack*. Listen and note what's wrong (in English), and the French words he uses to ask to change it.

Expressing your opinion

1 1•59 Listen to the key language:

Qu'est-ce que tu penses de ...?	What do you think of ...?
Il/Elle me va?	Does it suit me?
À mon avis ...	In my opinion ...
Il est trop long/court/sombre.	It's too long/short/dark.
Lequel/Laquelle tu préfères?	Which one (m/f) do you prefer?
Celui-ci, celle-là.	This one (m), that one (f).

To avoid repeating a noun, you can use:

lequel (m), **laquelle** (f)	*which one?*
celui-ci (m), **celle-ci** (f)	*this one*
celui-là (m), **celle-là** (f)	*that one*

Regarde ces pulls. Lequel tu préfères? Je préfère celui-ci.
Regarde ces chemises. Laquelle tu aimes? J'aime bien celle-là. **G8**

2 1•60 Vincent is buying a suit for a job interview with his girlfriend Gabrielle. Listen and tick the items of clothing as you hear them.

3 1•60 Listen again then fill the gaps using the words in the box.

ce	celle	ces	lequel	celui	laquelle

- Qu'est-ce que tu penses de .... costume? Il me va?

◆ À mon avis, la veste est un peu trop grande et elle est trop longue. Et puis, je n'aime pas la couleur; le noir, c'est trop sombre. Moi, j'aime ....-là, le bleu. Mais toi, ... tu préfères?

- Moi, j'aime bien ....-ci , en gris. Il est classe, et, en plus, il est confortable. Le bleu n'est pas très confortable. À ton avis, le pantalon gris n'est pas un peu trop court?

◆ Non, il est parfait. Bon, c'est décidé, on prend le gris. Maintenant il faut choisir une chemise. Alors, qu'est-ce que tu penses de .... chemises? .... tu préfères?

- J'aime bien ....-ci. Elle fait chic!

... and making comparisons

4   **1•61** Listen to the key language:

Je préfère le vert/la verte.	I prefer the green one.
Le bleu est plus pratique.	The blue one's more practical.
Il est plus facile à coordonner.	It's easier to match.
Il est moins cher que celui-là.	It's cheaper than that one (m).

> To compare things, you use **plus** *more* or **moins** *less* with an adjective: **plus pratique** *more practical*, **plus moulant** *more clingy*, **moins confortable** *less comfortable*.
>
> *Than* is **que**: **le bleu est moins cher que le vert** *the blue one is cheaper than the green one.*
>
> • Add **le** or **la** to describe something as *the most* ...:
> c'est <u>le</u> plus beau/<u>la</u> plus belle *it's the nicest (m/f).*   **G10**

En français

5   **1•62** It's now Gabrielle's turn to shop. She's trying on two sleeveless tops (**débardeurs**), one blue and one green, and shows them off to Vincent. Listen then jot down in English the pros and cons of each top.

- ◆ Alors, lequel tu préfères? Le bleu ou le vert?
- ● Hmm ... le bleu est plus pratique et il est plus facile à coordonner.
- ◆ Pour moi, le plus beau, c'est le vert: il est plus moulant, plus sexy.
- ● Ben, oui, mais il est trop court, tu ne trouves pas? Il est moins confortable. Je prends le bleu. Il coûte combien? Montre-moi l'étiquette ... Super, il est moins cher que le vert.

6   Make two sentences for each pair below, using **plus** and **moins**. The first is done for you.

- a **le lin / la laine – (en été) confortable**
  En été, le lin est plus confortable que la laine.
  En été, la laine est moins confortable que le lin.
- b **le cachemire / le coton – cher**
- c **le polyester / le cachemire – facile à laver**
- d **le coton / la soie – pratique**
- e **la soie / le coton – moulant**

put it all together

1   Match the nouns a–d with their adjectives 1–4.

a	chemise	1	noires
b	bottes	2	chers
c	pantalon	3	gris
d	tee-shirts	4	blanche

2   Choose the correct word from the list to complete each sentence.

> lequel   quelle   laquelle   celui   celles

a   La grise ou la bleue – .... préférez-vous?
b   Vous prenez quel tee-shirt? Le blanc ou le rose?
   Je prends ....-ci.
c   Vous faites .... taille, monsieur?
d   Vous voulez ....? Je prends le rouge, s'il vous plaît.
e   Je cherche des bottes noires. Je peux essayer ....-là?

3   Rewrite these sentences, replacing the shaded part with a word for *it* or *them* and changing the word order as necessary.

a   Je prends les bottes noires.
b   Yves cherche son sac à dos.
c   On peut laver la soie à la machine?
d   Nous regardons les chemises.
e   Est-ce que je peux échanger ce jean?
f   Tu aimes ces tee-shirts?

4   How would you say you're looking for the following items?

● a white cotton shirt
● jeans in size 38
● a blue jacket, pure wool, size 40
● a lightweight rucksack

1 **1•63** You're out shopping for clothes.

- **Je peux vous aider?**
- ◆ Say you're looking for a jacket.
- **Vous faites quelle taille?**
- ◆ Say you're a size 46.
- **Bon, nous avons des vestes en coton, lin, viscose, polyester, jean – ou peut-être voulez-vous une veste en laine?**
- ◆ Say yes, you'd like a wool jacket.
- **De quelle couleur?**
- ◆ Say you don't know – black or grey.
- **Nous avons une veste grise en pure laine, ou celle-ci, noire, en laine et cachemire.**
- ◆ Ask if you can try the black one on.
- **Oui ... Elle vous va très bien. Elle est très élégante.**
- ◆ Ask how much it costs.
- **Elle n'est pas très chère – trois cent quatre-vingt-dix euros.**

2 **1•64** On to another shop to change **un portefeuille** *a wallet*.

- ◆ Tell the assistant that there's a problem with this wallet.
- **Quel problème?**
- ◆ Say the zip's broken and you'd like to change it.
- **Malheureusement, je n'ai plus de portefeuilles comme ça. Mais j'ai celui-ci. Il vous plaît?**
- ◆ You're not sure. Ask your friend what she thinks of this one.
- **À mon avis, il est un peu trop petit.**

3 **1•65** To a third shop where your friend tries on a jumper.

- **Tu aimes ce pull? Il me va?** *Does it suit me?*
- ◆ You think it's hideous. Say, in your opinion, it's a bit too short.
- **Tu crois? Moi, je l'aime beaucoup, et il y a une réduction de 25% (vingt-cinq pour cent).**
- ◆ You find a different jumper. Tell her you prefer this one ... and it's less expensive.
- **Ah oui, il est super, merci!**

quiz

1 Which is the odd one out: **laine**, **soie**, **léger**, **coton**?

2 How do you say *I'm looking for...*? What's the infinitive of this verb?

3 **Taille** and **pointure** both mean *size*, but when do you use each one?

4 How would you say something is too expensive?

5 To say *this jacket*, would you use **ce** or **cette**?

6 What's the missing word in this sentence? **La chemise est moins chère .... la veste.**

7 If you say *I'll take this one*, referring to a backpack, how will you say *this one*?

8 What's the French for a zip?

Now check whether you can ...

- say what you're looking for in a shop
- use adjectives to describe something
- express your opinion and ask for someone else's
- compare things using **plus** and **moins (que)**
- differentiate between *this one* and *that one*, and ask *which one?*
- use *it* and *them* in the correct position
- express a preference

Being able to give an opinion in a new language is a great step forward. Get used to saying in French what you think: comment on the news using **à mon avis** and adjectives such as **fantastique**, **extraordinaire**, **tragique** or **absurde**, or, more colloquially, **génial**, **cool**, **nul** or **dégoûtant**.

Try commenting on the contents of your wardrobe: describing your clothes as **long** or **court**, comparing them using **plus** and **moins**, and perhaps evaluating them as **idéal**, **parfait**, **pratique** or **horrible**!

J'ai perdu mon ordinateur portable

asking the way

... and following directions

explaining what's happened

reporting a problem

En France ...

if you lose your **portefeuille** *wallet/purse* or your **ordinateur portable** *laptop*, you'll need to **faire une déclaration à la police** *report the incident to the police*. To do so, find the nearest **commissariat de police** *police station*. France has two law-enforcement agencies. **La police**, who are part of the Ministry of the Interior, tend to be in charge in urban areas, whereas in rural France you're more likely to deal with **la gendarmerie**, who are under the auspices of the Ministry of Defence. In the case of an emergency, ring 17 from a telephone (landline) or 112 from a mobile.

Asking the way

1   2•1 Listen to the key language:

Vous pouvez nous/m'aider?	Can you help us/me?
Pour aller à …?	How do I/we get to …?
Continuez …	Continue/Keep going …
(Vous) tournez …	(You) turn …
Vous devez prendre …	You have to take …

2   2•2 Jack and his wife Niamh are looking for the **commissariat** to report a lost **ordinateur portable** *laptop*. The directions a passer-by gives them include some of the following phrases. Read the lists, then listen and tick the phrases you hear.

tournez à gauche *turn left*	**vous passez devant la gare routière** *you pass the bus station*
à droite *on the right*	**vous traversez un pont** *you cross a bridge*
tout droit *straight ahead*	**devant** *by, in front of*
jusqu'au bout de la rue *to the end of the street*	**tout près** *very close*
jusqu'aux feux *as far as the lights*	**à côté d'un collège** *next to a school*
jusqu'au carrefour *as far as the crossroads*	**en face d'un collège** *opposite a school*

3   2•3 In reply to **Vous avez compris?** *Have you understood?* Jack repeats the directions they've been given. Listen and spot his two mistakes.

... and following directions

4 2•4 On the way, Jack needs to **retirer de l'argent** *withdraw some cash* and asks a passer-by for the nearest **distributeur de billets** *cashpoint*. Listen and find it on this map.

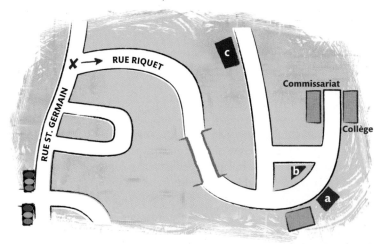

5 2•5 Listen to the key language:

Le/La ..., c'est bien par ici?	Is this the way to the ...?
Vous vous trompez de direction.	You're going in the wrong direction.
L'arrêt est ici.	The bus stop is here.
Vous devez descendre ...	You have to get off (the bus) ...

6 2•6 Niamh decides to ask someone else if they're going the right way to the **commissariat**. Listen and see if you can summarise the reply:

a The police station is quite ....
b They can catch the number .... bus.
c They have to get off at the .... bus stop.
d It's only .... minutes.
e The police station is located ....

Explaining what's happened

1 **2•7** Listen to the key language:

J'ai perdu ...	I've lost ...
Je n'ai pas entendu.	I didn't hear.
Qu'est-ce que tu as dit?	What did you say?
On m'a volé mon ordinateur portable.	Someone has stolen my laptop.
Tu as fait une déclaration à la police?	Have you reported it?

En français

To talk about the past, e.g. to say *I lost*, *I've lost* or *Did you lose ...?*, you use the present tense of **avoir** and the past participle (pp) of the main verb. This is called the perfect tense. For regular verbs, the pp is formed by changing **-er** to **-é** and **-re** to **-u**:

trouver ▸ trouvé	j'ai trouvé *I found*
perdre ▸ perdu	j'ai perdu *I lost*

Vous avez trouvé ...? *Did you find ...?/Have you found ...?*

The past participles of many common verbs are irregular:

dire ▸ dit	faire ▸ fait	comprendre ▸ compris	**G22**

2 **2•8** Jack rings their friend Colette to explain why they're running late. Listen, then fit these past participles in the right places. One is used twice.

- Bonjour, Colette, c'est moi, Jack.
- Salut, Jack. Ça va?

volé	entendu
perdu	dit fait

- Non, ça ne va pas très bien. J'ai .... mon ordinateur portable.
- Comment? Je n'ai pas .... Qu'est-ce que tu as ....?
- J'ai .... mon ordinateur portable! Enfin, on m'a .... mon ordinateur portable!
- Ah, c'est pas possible! Tu as .... une déclaration à la police? Tu dois aller tout de suite au commissariat.
- Oui, oui, on y va maintenant.
- Allez, bon courage! À plus tard.

3 **2•9** Jack also rings their friend François to say they're **en retard** *running late*. Can you work out why Niamh's irritated?

Reporting a problem

1 2•10 Listen to the key language:

Qu'est-ce qui est arrivé?	What happened?
j'ai mis	I put
j'ai bu	I drank
j'ai lu	I read
Vous avez vu quelqu'un?	Did you see anyone?
Je n'ai vu personne.	I didn't see anyone.

2 2•11 At the **commissariat**, the **agent de police** takes a statement. As well as **commandé** *ordered*, it includes **vu**, **lu**, **bu** and **mis**, the irregular past participles of **voir** *to see*, **lire** *to read*, **boire** *to drink* and **mettre** *to put*. Listen to Jack's statement, then number these events 1–7 in the order they happened.

  a J'ai lu mon journal.
  b J'ai mis mon portefeuille dans ma poche.
  c J'ai cherché mon ordinateur portable.
  d J'ai payé.
  e J'ai bu mon café.
  f J'ai mis mon ordinateur portable par terre.
  g J'ai commandé un café au lait.
  h Je n'ai pas trouvé mon ordinateur.

3 Now imagine you witnessed what happened at the café, and describe what Jack did, starting with **Il a mis son ordinateur portable** ....

When making a perfect tense negative, **ne** and **pas** go round just the **avoir** part: Je **n'**ai **pas** bu mon café. *I didn't drink my coffee.*

● Some other negatives behave in the same way – **ne ... rien** *nothing* and **ne ... jamais** *never*:

Je **n'**ai **rien** vu. *I didn't see anything.*

Je **n'**ai **jamais** lu *Le Monde*. *I've never read Le Monde.*

● But **ne ... personne** *no-one* goes round the whole perfect tense:

Je **n'**ai vu **personne**. *I didn't see anyone.*

G27

En français

put it all together

1 Look at the French phrases. Which one would you use:

1 Qu'est-ce qui est arrivé?

2 Qu'est-ce que vous avez vu?

3 Vous avez vu quelqu'un?

4 Vous pouvez nous aider?

5 Je n'ai pas compris.

  a to ask someone if they've seen somebody?

  b to ask someone to help you and your friends?

  c to ask what's happened?

  d to say you haven't understood?

  e to ask someone what they've seen?

2 Using the verbs in the box, how would you say these in French?

  a I've lost my passport.
  b Have you (**tu**) ordered a coffee?
  c Did you (**vous**) understand the guide?
  d Niamh has booked a table.
  e Have you (**vous**) heard?
  f They've reported the incident.
  g She didn't see anyone.
  h He visited the museum.

commander
faire
réserver
visiter
entendre
perdre
comprendre
voir

3 A friend left you this list of jobs. Write a note to tell him which you've done (✓) and which you haven't (✗), e.g: **j'ai réservé une table au restaurant pour ce soir**; **je n'ai pas acheté Le Monde**.

S'il te plaît, aujourd'hui, tu peux ...?
réserver une table au restaurant pour ce soir (✓)
acheter le journal Le Monde (✗)
inviter Nathalie au restaurant (✓)
acheter du pain (✓)
mettre le linge dans la machine à laver (✓)
téléphoner à Robert (✗)
retirer de l'argent (✗)

1   2•12 You and your partner need to get to the police station.

- Stop a man in the street and ask if he can help you.
- ◆ **Oui, bien sûr. Vous avez un problème?**
- Ask how to get to the police station.
- ◆ **C'est assez loin – rue St-Germain. Vous devez prendre l'autobus numéro seize.**
- After a short bus ride, you still can't find it, so ask a woman if this is the right way to the police station.
- ◆ **Oui, continuez tout droit, et tournez à droite après les feux. Le commissariat se trouve à gauche en face d'un supermarché.**
- Thank her.

2   Now translate for your partner how to get to the police station.

3   2•13 Paul Bauchet, a colleague, leaves you a message saying there's a problem and to call him. You know him well so use **tu**.

- **Allô! Paul Bauchet.**
- ◆ Ask him what's happened.
- **J'ai perdu ...**
- ◆ You didn't catch that, so ask what he said.
- **J'ai perdu mon portefeuille. Je l'ai perdu au bureau hier. Tu l'as vu?**
- ◆ Say yes, Stéphane found a wallet at the office. A black wallet.
- **Ah, oui! Ça doit être mon portefeuille. Merci! Et vous deux, qu'est-ce que vous avez fait aujourd'hui?**
- ◆ Say you visited the castle. (Use **on**.)
- **Et vous avez déjeuné où?**
- ◆ Say you had lunch in a small restaurant in the town centre.
- **Très bien!**

quiz

1 What are the emergency phone numbers in France?

2 Can you give the French for *station*, *bus station* and *police station*?

3 What's the difference between **tout droit** and **à droite**?

4 If somebody says to you **Vous avez compris?**, what do they want to know?

5 What do you think **vous vous trompez de numéro** means?

6 How would you ask if this is the right way to the bank?

7 On a bus, to ask where you have to get off, you'd say: **Je dois .... où?**

8 If **acheter** is *to buy* and **vendre** is *to sell*, how do you say *I bought* and *I sold*?

Now check whether you can ...

- ask the way to a particular place
- follow instructions to get there
- say what you've done
- say what someone else has done

You've passed the half-way mark in *Talk French 2* – a good time to bring together some of the vocabulary from the six units you've covered. For example:

- say what time you had lunch and dinner yesterday (**hier**) using the perfect tense of **déjeuner** *to have lunch* or **dîner** *to have dinner/ supper*.
- say what you watched on television and listened to on the radio yesterday, using **regarder ... à la télévision** and **écouter ... à la radio**.

1 Read the statement Colette Berthier made after losing her handbag, then find ten mistakes that somehow made their way into the official **déclaration de perte** *loss report*.

Je m'appelle Colette Berthier. J'habite à Lyon, 29 rue Sainte-Thérèse. J'ai trente et un ans: je suis née à Toulon en 1976.

Hier soir, mardi 20 mars, je suis allée au complexe sportif, place de la Victoire. J'ai mis mon sac à main sur un banc au fond de la salle. La classe a fini à vingt heures et après j'ai parlé avec quelques amies pendant cinq ou six minutes. Je crois que quelqu'un a pris mon sac pendant ce temps-là, mais je n'ai rien vu.

Mon sac est assez petit, en cuir marron. Il a coûté cent vingt euros. Dans le sac, il y a mon portable, mon portefeuille qui contient environ trente ou trente-cinq euros, ma carte de crédit, ma carte d'abonné et une photo de mon mari.

---

cuir *leather*　　**marron** *brown*　　**la carte d'abonné** *season ticket*

Nom: Berthier
Prénom: Josette
Adresse: 29 place Sainte-Thérèse
Né(e) à: Toulouse

Circonstances de la perte

Date: mercredi 21 mars
Heure: 19h00
Où: complexe culturel
Description: sac de sport marron, contenant: portable, €120, carte d'identité, deux photos

Only can be expressed by putting **ne** and **que** around the verb:
Je **n'**ai **que** dix euros. *I've only got €10.*
Je **n'**ai payé **que** vingt euros. *I paid only €20.*

Note that ne ... que, like ne ... **personne**, goes around both parts of a perfect tense verb.

Remember, other negatives just go round the auxiliary verb (avoir/être):
Je **n'**ai **pas** acheté de veste. *I didn't buy a jacket.*
On **n'a** **rien** vu. *We didn't see anything.*
Je **n'**ai **jamais** vu ce film. *I've never seen that film.*
Il **n'a** **plus** parlé avec moi. *He didn't talk to me any more.*

G27

2 Gabrielle e-mails her friend, Sylvie, to tell her about Vincent's interview. First read it straight through to see if you can get an overall impression, then use the glossary to help you with the questions on the next page.

-----Message original-----
De: Gabrielle Masson **Date:** vendredi 18 mai, 18:46
À: Sylvie Chevalier **Objet:** nouvelles!

Salut, Sylvie!
On a passé tout l'après-midi en ville et je suis fatiguée. Moi, je n'ai acheté qu'un débardeur. J'ai eu de la chance, je l'ai acheté en solde. Il ressemble un peu à celui que tu as acheté en Espagne.

Vincent a trouvé un costume et une chemise. Il a un entretien la semaine prochaine avec une société qui fait du commerce avec l'Amérique du Sud. Génial, non? Il a fait un séjour au Brésil, mais il n'a jamais été dans les autres pays d'Amérique latine. Il cherche depuis quelques mois un emploi moins stressant, avec un chef plus sympa.

Il a vu l'annonce dans un journal (j'ai oublié lequel), le week-end dernier. Lundi, il a téléphoné à la société et mercredi, il a reçu une lettre l'invitant à passer un entretien.

Toi aussi, tu as eu des entretiens dans des collèges, non? Lequel tu préfères? Celui où Amina travaille?
Voilà, je n'ai plus de nouvelles. À bientôt!
Gabi

3 **Vrai ou faux?** Then correct the false statements.

	vrai	faux
a Gabrielle a acheté un débardeur en Espagne.	☐	☐
b Le débardeur a coûté moins cher que son prix normal.	☐	☐
c Gabrielle veut changer d'emploi.	☐	☐
d Vincent a déjà fait un séjour en Amérique du Sud.	☐	☐
e Le chef de Vincent est très sympa.	☐	☐
f Sylvie a un entretien la semaine prochaine.	☐	☐
g Amina travaille dans un collège.	☐	☐

4 Find ten different past participles in the e-mail, including three new irregular ones from **recevoir**, **être** and **avoir**.

5 Imagine you're Sylvie. Compose a message to Gabrielle:

- thank her for her e-mail;
- say you've never visited South America;
- tell her you've had three interviews, you prefer the Collège Jeanne d'Arc – it's further away than Amina's college but the other teachers are nicer;
- say you've no more news.

The second word of some negative expressions can occur alone to answer a question:

Qu'est-ce que tu fais? *Rien! What are you doing? Nothing!*

Tu te lèves tôt le week-end? Jamais! *Do you get up early at weekends? Never!*

Qui as-tu vu? Personne! *Who did you see? No-one.*

En français

---

6 Choose the response which best answers the question.

- **Vous mangez de la viande?**
  Jamais! / Personne! / Rien!
- **Qui parle russe dans la société?**
  Jamais. / Personne. / Rien.
- **Tu as vu quelque chose?**
  Non, je n'ai jamais vu ça. / Non, je n'ai vu personne. / Non, je n'ai rien vu.
- **Vous avez acheté deux chemises?**
  Non, je n'ai acheté que deux chemises. / Non, je n'aime pas mes chemises. / Non, je n'ai acheté qu'une chemise.

7 Read about some new and secondhand objects made of leather for sale online. Use the glossary to help you match up the adverts with the items listed in the box.

gants   collier   étui   ceinture   blouson   sac de voyage

a
Conception élégante et d'excellente qualité, de couleur rose, ... fin et léger convient parfaitement à votre portable. Bouton magnétique pour ouvrir et fermer, facile à utiliser.

b
Fantastiques .... en cuir et fourrure de lapin gris clair pour gardez les mains au chaud pendant tout l'hiver. Taille unique.

c
.... homme en cuir de buffle véritable. Style motard. Neuf avec étiquette. Produit de très bonne qualité. Longueur 70 cm, manches 65 cm.

d
Très beau .... en cuir. Dimensions: 50 x 26 x 35 cm. 2 compartiments à l'intérieur, 1 pochette avec fermeture éclair, 1 pochette téléphone. Fabriqué en France, c'est un modèle à ne pas rater!!

e
.... homme ajustable, cuir glacé marron foncé. Longeur de l'attache au dernier trou: 88cm, largeur: 4,5 cm. Comme neuve.

f
Superbe .... de chien, cuir noir, pour chien de taille moyenne. Largeur 3 cm, longueur 55 cm, tour de cou 40 cm à 50 cm. Tout neuf.

Vous êtes allé où?

talking about your holiday plans

saying what the weather's like

talking about past holidays

... and saying what you did

En France ...

the fine cuisine, agreeable climate and proximity to wonderful locations mean that many French people prefer to spend their **vacances** *holidays* in France rather than going abroad. Many choose to go **à la montagne** *to the mountains* or **au bord de la mer** *to the seaside*. Large cities can become very quiet in the second half of July and throughout August as the great exodus takes place. Some companies close down for the period. Throughout the rest of the year, the French like to get away too and will often **faire le pont** which means taking days off between the weekend and a mid-week public holiday to give an extended break.

Talking about your holiday plans

1 2•14 Listen to the key language:

Vous allez où en vacances?	Where are you going on holiday?
cette année/cet été	this year/this summer
Je vais en/à/au ...	I'm going to ...
Je vais aller en Bretagne.	I'm going to go to Brittany.
Je reste à la maison.	I'm staying at home.
comme d'habitude	as usual

2 2•15 In a **sondage** *survey* people are asked where they're going on holiday this year. Read these replies, then listen and tick those you hear. (See page 23 to remind yourself how to say 'to' places. Note that *to the south of France* is **dans le Midi**.)

☐ **Nous allons au bord de la mer avec nos enfants.**
☐ **On va dans le Midi, comme d'habitude.**
☐ **Je vais en Provence avec des amis.**
☐ **Je vais au Pays Basque, dans un petit village ...**
☐ **Je reste à la maison.**
☐ **Je vais aller en Bretagne, cet été ...**
☐ **Je vais en Corse avec mes parents.**
☐ **On va à la montagne, près de la frontière espagnole.**

En français

Aller *to go* is a key irregular verb:

je vais	tu vas	il/elle/on va
nous allons	vous allez	ils/elles vont

It's used very much as in English – either to talk about going to a place: **Tu vas où? Je vais en Corse** *Where are you going? I'm going to Corsica*, or to say what you're going to do in the near future: **Je vais voir des amis** *I'm going to see friends*.

G17

3 2•16 Here's the full reply from someone who's heading off **toute seule** *on her own*. Listen then fill the gaps with the right forms of **aller**.
- ● Excusez-moi, vous .... où en vacances, cette année?
- ◆ Cette année, je vais .... en Provence – toute seule! Je suis divorcée et ma fille .... en vacances avec son père. Ils .... en Martinique.

Saying what the weather's like

soleil

brouillard

vent fort

pluie

neige

orage

nuages

éclaircies

averses

En français

Both **il y a** and **il fait** appear in weather expressions:

Il y a du soleil/du vent/de l'orage/des nuages. It's sunny/windy/stormy/cloudy.

Il fait quel temps? What's the weather like?

Il fait beau/mauvais. It's fine/bad weather.

Il fait chaud/froid. It's hot/cold.

To refer to the past, **il fait** becomes **il a fait**:

Il a fait très beau. The weather was lovely.

1   **2•17** Arnaud, who's going to the Basque Country, describes the weather there. Listen and jot down in English what he says. See if you can also catch what the average temperature is in July and August.

En juillet et en août, la température moyenne est de .... degrés.

Talking about past holidays

1 2•18 Listen to the key language:

Tu es allé(e) où?	Where did you go?
l'année dernière	last year
l'été dernier	last summer
il y a deux ans	two years ago
Des amis sont venus.	Some friends came.
On est restés chez nous.	We stayed at home.

You form the perfect tense of a few verbs with **être** not **avoir**, e.g. **aller** *to go*, **rester** *to stay*, **arriver** *to arrive*, **partir** *to depart*, **venir** *to come*. With these, the ending of the pp agrees with the subject:

je suis allé (m)	je suis allée (f)
Thomas est parti	Émilie est partie
les garçons sont arrivés	les filles sont arrivées

The spelling of the pp with **vous** depends on who you're talking to:
Vous êtes allé/allée où? (one man/one woman)
Vous êtes allés où? (a group of men or a mixed group)
Vous êtes allées où? (a group of women)

G24

2 2•19 People are also asked where they went on holiday last year. Before you listen, read the replies, and work out the gender of each speaker and whether they're talking about one or more people.

a Je suis allée au bord de la mer.
b Je suis allé à Biarritz, comme d'habitude.
c Je suis allé sur la côte ouest de l'Irlande.
d L'été dernier, nous sommes allés dans le Midi, à St-Tropez.
e Je suis allé en Guadeloupe pour voir mes parents.
f On n'est pas partis en vacances, l'année dernière.

3 In French, how would …

- a man say *I went to Corsica with my girlfriend* (**ma copine**)?
- two women say *We went to Martinique last year*? (use **on**)
- a couple say *We went to Ireland with friends*? (use **nous**)
- a woman say *I went to Paris two years ago*?

... and saying what you did

4 2●20 Listen to the key language.

On est partis de la maison à ...	We left home at ...
On est arrivés à ...	We arrived at ...
On est rentrés vers ...	We got back at about ...
Qu'est-ce que vous y avez fait?	What did you do there?

5 2●21 Arnaud is at work on Monday morning. Listen as a colleague asks whether he had a good weekend. Try to catch where he went and with whom.

Où? ....   **Avec qui?** ....

En français

Monter *to climb/go up* and **descendre** *to go down/get off a train or bus* also form the perfect tense with **être**.

The spelling of the pp (past participle) with **on** depends on who **on** refers to:

on est montés (a group of men or a mixed group)

on est descendues (a group of women)   **G24**

---

6 2●22 Arnaud goes on to describe his day in Brussels. He was particularly impressed with the futuristic science centre **l'Atomium**, built to resemble an iron molecule. Before you listen, read the jumbled-up version of events and number them in the order you predict they occurred.

  a Après ça, on est allés à l'Atomium.
  b Vers neuf heures et quart, on est arrivés à Bruxelles.
  c On y a déjeuné.
  d On est rentrés à Paris vers dix heures du soir.
  e On est partis de la maison vers sept heures du matin.
  f On est montés dans la sphère la plus haute, où il y a un restaurant.
  g On est descendus par les escalators.
  h D'abord, on est allés à la Grand-Place.

put it all together

1   Match the symbols and the phrases.

a

d

b

2°

e 40°

c

f

1   Il fait mauvais temps.

2   Il fait très chaud.

3   Il y a du soleil.

4   Il y a des nuages.

5   Il fait froid.

6   Il neige.

2   Fill the gaps with the right part of the present tense of **aller**.

   a   Tu .... où en vacances, cette année?
   b   Nous .... en Irlande.
   c   Vous .... comment au travail? En train ou en voiture?
   d   Je .... au cinéma ce soir.
   e   Olivier et Magali .... au bord de la mer.
   f   On .... où, cet après-midi?
   g   Ariane .... dans le Midi, en juillet.
   h   Moi, j'y .... toute seule.

3   Rewrite this paragraph as if it happened last year instead of this year. Begin: **L'année dernière, ...**

   Cette année, je vais en vacances en Corse avec des amis. On part en bateau de Marseille, et on arrive à Bastia, en Corse. Il fait très chaud là-bas. On va faire du ski nautique.

4   Give these replies to the question **Vous allez où en vacances?**

   a   I'm going to the seaside.
   b   We (**nous**) are going to the South of France (**Midi**) with the family.
   c   I'm going to go to the west coast of Ireland with friends.
   d   We (**on**) aren't going on holiday this year, we're staying at home.

1   2•23 A French friend coming to the UK phones to ask what the weather's like.

- **Dis-moi: il fait quel temps?**
- ◆ Tell him the weather's good; it's sunny.
- **Il ne fait pas froid?**
- ◆ Say no, it's 21°.

2   2•24 Now to talk about your holiday plans.

a
- **Tu vas où en vacances cette année?**
- ◆ Say you're going to Italy.
- **Tu y vas seul(e)?**
- ◆ Say no, you're going with friends.

b
- **Vous allez en France cette année?**
- ◆ Say yes, you're going to go to Provence with your partner (**mon compagnon/ma compagne**).
- **C'est une belle région! Vous allez à la montagne ou au bord de la mer?**
- ◆ Say to the mountains, and explain that your cousin (**cousin**) has a gîte near Gordes.
- **Ah, c'est super! C'est un très joli village.**

3   2•25 Now some questions about your holiday last summer.

- **Vous êtes allé(e) où, l'été dernier?**
- ◆ Say you went to Brittany. Add that you went with friends.
- **Vous y êtes allés en voiture, ou en train?**
- ◆ Say you went by train (use **on**).
- **Il a fait quel temps?**
- ◆ Say it was quite warm, 22°.

4   How would you yourself reply to these questions?

- **Vous allez où en vacances cette année?**
- **Vous êtes allé(e) où en vacances l'année dernière?**
- **Et il y a deux ans, vous êtes allé(e) où?**

quiz

1 What word means both *midday* and *the South of France*?

2 What's the French equivalent of *to make a long weekend of it* – **faire le ...**?

3 To ask a friend where he or she is going on holiday, do you need **vais**, **vas**, **va** or **vont**?

4 Can you think of two verbs beginning with **a** that use **être** to form the perfect tense?

5 How would you say *ten years ago* in French?

6 How do you say in French that the weather's bad?

7 What's the difference between **il fait chaud** and **il a fait chaud**?

8 Given that **tomber** *to fall* uses **être** to form the perfect tense, how would you say *I fell*?

Now check whether you can ...

- use **aller** to say where you and other people are going
- talk about holiday plans: where you're going and who with
- say that you're going to go somewhere
- talk about past holidays: say where you went and what you did
- comment on the weather

Now that you know how to talk about the past, you could either keep a simple diary in French or talk (to yourself or anyone who'll listen and understand!) about what you've been doing. Keep it simple and repetitive at first, sticking to **je suis allé(e)** and using **partir**, **arriver**, **rester** and **sortir** with the time of day. If keeping a diary, record the weather, using **il a fait ....**

Je ne vais pas bien

saying how you're feeling

relating an incident

describing symptoms

following instructions

En France ...

médecin is the word usually used to mean 'doctor' and applies to both male and female doctors. When addressing doctors, you call them **Docteur**. There's also the colloquial **toubib**, which has been borrowed from Arabic. French citizens have access to **la Sécurité sociale** *the National Health Service* on production of their **carte vitale**, a medical identity card which can store important information. Patients have to pay for their health treatment and get part of the costs reimbursed later. EU citizens can make use of the health service provided they have a European Health Insurance Card (EHIC). In an emergency, dial 15 for the nearest **Service d'Aide Médicale d'Urgence (SAMU)** unit, the special emergency service unit.

Saying how you're feeling

1   **2•26** Listen to the key language.

Qu'est-ce que tu as?	What's the matter with you?
Tu as eu un accident?	Have you had an accident?
Je ne vais pas bien du tout.	I'm not well at all.
Je suis malade.	I'm ill.
J'ai mal partout.	I'm aching all over.
Je peux à peine marcher.	I can hardly walk.

2   Read this message from Élodie to her friend Camille. Why can't she meet her at lunchtime?

> salut, ne peux pas te rencontrer à midi. ne vais pas au travail aujourd'hui. suis malade. désolée. Élodie

Aller is used to talk about health, where in English we use *to be*:

Comment vas-tu/allez-vous? *How are you?*

Je ne vais pas bien. *I'm not well.*   **Il va mieux.** *He's feeling better.*

3   **2•27** Camille rings Élodie to find out what's wrong. First listen to their conversation. Then fill the gaps, and listen once more to check. **On se retrouve demain?** *Shall we meet up tomorrow?*

- ● Élodie, tu ne .... pas bien?
- ◆ Non, je suis malade. Je ne vais pas .... du tout.
- ● Ma pauvre! Qu'est-ce que tu as?
- ◆ J'ai .... partout. Je peux à peine marcher.
- ● Quoi! C'est affreux! Tu .... eu un accident?
- ◆ Non, non. Hier, Michel et moi, on .... allés à la montagne – on .... fait cent kilomètres!
- ● Élodie, n'exagère pas!
- ◆ D'accord, dix kilomètres. Et moi, je .... tombée! J'ai eu peur!

4   Write an e-mail to Sandrine, a mutual friend, saying Élodie isn't going into work today, she's not feeling well. She went to the mountains with Michel yesterday, she fell over and she's aching all over.

Relating an incident

1 2•28 Listen to the key language:

On s'est promenés.	We went for a walk.
il s'est arrêté	he stopped
elle s'est arrêtée	she stopped
elle s'est reposée	she had a rest
elle ne s'est pas fait mal	she didn't hurt herself
on s'est retrouvés	we met up
Je me suis bien amusé(e).	I enjoyed myself.

All reflexive verbs (**se lever**, **se reposer**, etc.) form the perfect tense with **être**. Just as for **aller** or **sortir**, the pp agrees with the subject, adding **-e** and/or **-s** as required:

je me suis reposé(e)

tu t'es reposé(e)

il s'est reposé, elle s'est reposée

on s'est reposé(e)(s)

nous nous sommes reposé(e)s

vous vous êtes reposé(e)(s)

ils se sont reposés, elles se sont reposées   **G25**

En français

---

2 2•29 Michel tells his friend Julien about his day out yesterday. Read and listen to his version of accounts, which is somewhat different from Élodie's. Pick out seven reflexive verbs in the perfect tense. **À mi-chemin** is *half way*.

Hier, Élodie et moi, on s'est promenés à la campagne. Je pense qu'elle s'est bien amusée. Moi, en tout cas, je me suis bien amusé. Je suis monté jusqu'au sommet d'une belle petite colline. Élodie s'est arrêtée à mi-chemin et elle s'est reposée. On s'est retrouvés plus tard pour descendre. Elle est tombée une fois, mais heureusement, elle ne s'est pas fait mal.

3 **a** If Michel had stopped and had a rest, how would he say so?
  b How would he say they both had a good time (using first **nous** and then **on**)?

Describing symptoms

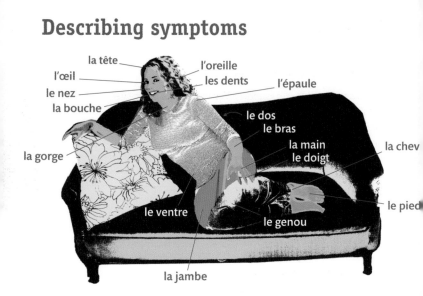

la tête
l'oreille
l'œil
les dents
l'épaule
le nez
la bouche
le dos
le bras
la main
la chev
le doigt
la gorge
le ventre
le genou
le pied
la jambe

The plural of **l'œil** is very irregular – **les yeux** – and the plural of **le genou** adds an –**x** – **les genoux**.

To say something hurts, aches or is sore, you need the phrase **avoir mal à ...** Remember that **à** can't be followed by **le** or **les** – it becomes **au** and **aux** respectively: **j'ai mal à la gorge, elle a mal au ventre, mon fils a mal aux dents.**

1   2•30 Camille rings Élodie again later. Listen and spot which parts of her Élodie says hurt.

2   2•31 Élodie phones her sister Fabienne hoping for a bit of sympathy, but Fabienne can't talk at the moment because her little boy Théo is ill. Read this list of potential symptoms, listen to Fabienne, then tick the ones Théo's displaying.

il a mal à l'oreille	**il a mal aux dents**
il a mal à la gorge	**il a mal au dos**
il a mal à la tête	**il a mal au ventre**
il tousse *he's coughing*	
il a de la fièvre *he's got a temperature*	
il saigne du nez *he's got a nose-bleed*	

Following instructions

1   **2•32** Listen to the key language.

Vous pouvez plier le genou?	Can you bend your knee?
Ça fait mal.	It hurts.
Ce n'est pas grave.	It's not serious.
Prenez des ...	Take some ...
... analgésiques/comprimés.	... painkillers/tablets.
Reposez-vous.	Rest.
Ne vous inquiétez pas.	Don't worry.

2   **2•33** The next morning, Élodie hobbles to the doctor's. Here's an outline of their conversation for you to read with the aid of the glossary before you listen to it.

Her complaint:	**Je peux à peine marcher.**
His diagnosis:	**Une contusion, un petit bleu. Ce n'est pas grave.**
His advice:	**Prenez des analgésiques, reposez-vous et faites peu d'exercice.**

When telling someone to do something, you include **vous** with reflexive verbs. So it's

prenez *take*, faites *do*, ne buvez pas *don't drink*

BUT

reposez-vous *rest*, amusez-vous bien *enjoy yourself*,
ne vous inquiétez pas *don't worry*

G26

En français

---

3   **2•34** Élodie goes to the **pharmacie** for some painkillers. Listen and see if you can pick out and jot down any of the **pharmacien**'s instructions, based on what you might expect to hear in English in the same circumstances. Then check with the transcript on page 123.

put it all together

1   Find the odd one out in each line.

œil, bras, nez, oreille, bouche, dents
cheville, pied, genou, tête, jambe
toubib, médecin, pharmacien, docteur

2   Choose the correct ending for each sentence.

a	Théo a mal	1	bien.
b	Comment	2	amusés.
c	Je me suis	3	à la tête.
d	Qu'est-ce que	4	des analgésiques.
e	Je ne vais pas	5	allez-vous?
f	Prenez	6	reposée.
g	On s'est bien	7	tu as?

3   Write an e-mail in French (using **tu**) to your friend Antoine, telling him:

- you're sorry but you can't go to the cinema this evening,
- you're not at all well, you've got a temperature, your back and legs hurt,
- your husband/wife/partner has got a headache and a sore throat.

Also, ask him how he is and whether:

- he went to work today,
- he's seen Thomas.

De: Date:
À: Antoine de la Rochette   Objet: ce soir

1 2•35 Imagine you're Michel, Élodie's boyfriend. It's the day after your walk and you phone her.

- Say hello and ask if she's well.
- ◆ **Non, je ne vais pas bien du tout.**
- Ask what the matter is with her.
- ◆ **J'ai mal au dos, j'ai mal au genou. Je peux à peine marcher.**
- She clearly needs sympathy. Say **ma pauvre** (*you poor thing*) and ask if she's had an accident.
- ◆ **Un accident? Mais non! C'est la montagne – hier – tu comprends?**
- Say, but yesterday you went for a walk in the country.
- ◆ **Oui, on a fait vingt kilomètres et je suis tombée, et maintenant j'ai mal partout et je peux à peine marcher.**
- Tell her you walked five kilometres, then excuse yourself and say you've got a meeting in five minutes.

2 2•36 You're now going to describe a whole host of unpleasant symptoms of your own!

- **Comment vas-tu aujourd'hui?**
- ◆ Say you're not well.
- **Désolée. Qu'est-ce que tu as?**
- ◆ Say you've got a headache and a sore throat.
- **Mon pauvre!**
- ◆ And your back hurts.
- **Tu as de la fièvre?**
- ◆ Say yes, and you have a cough and you have earache.
- **À mon avis, tu as la grippe. Tu as pris quelque chose?**
- ◆ Say no, but you would like some painkillers.
- **J'en ai qui sont très efficaces. Attends une minute.**

quiz

1 What's the acronym for the French emergency mobile units? And what's the phone number for them?

2 How do you ask somebody (**tu**) what the matter is?

3 If you can hardly walk, what do you add to **je peux à** .... **marcher**?

4 What's the difference between **Elle va bien** and **Elle va mieux**?

5 How would you say in French that you've got a) stomach ache and b) a headache?

6 **Vous avez** .... **un accident?** What word do you need to add to ask somebody if they've had an accident?

7 In an accident situation, how would you say 'he's hurt himself'?

8 And how would you tell the injured person to rest and not to worry?

Now check whether you can ...

- say how you're feeling
- list simple symptoms, yours and other people's
- explain what hurts when you're in pain
- relate a sequence of events
- follow straightforward instructions from a doctor or chemist

If you're having difficulty understanding something in French, it can often help to imagine yourself in a similar situation in an English-speaking country and to think of the phrases you'd expect to hear there.

Nobody minds being asked to repeat something, so don't hesitate to say **Répétez, s'il vous plaît** or **Vous pouvez répéter?** Not only does it give you another chance to listen but, along with words like **Alors, Eh bien** or **Ben** *Well*, it provides useful thinking time.

Verbs which use **être** to form the perfect tense include **naître** (pp **né**) *to be born*, **mourir** (pp **mort**) *to die* and **rentrer** (pp **rentré**) *to return/come home*:

Elle est née en Écosse. *She was born in Scotland.*

Son mari est mort il y a cinq ans. *Her husband died five years ago.*

Nous sommes rentrés vers trois heures du matin. *We came home around 3am.*

G24

1   Complete each of Edith Moreau's sentences with the right part of **avoir** or **être**.

   a   La semaine dernière, j'............ écrit une lettre au journal régional.

   b   Ma petite-fille .... née à Grenoble, en 1991.

   c   Je me .... mariée quatre ans après la fin de la deuxième guerre mondiale.

   d   Mon mari .... mort, il y a trois ans.

   e   Je m'appelle Edith Moreau. Je .... née à Vittel, en 1930.

   f   Hier, le facteur .... apporté deux réponses à ma lettre.

   g   Il y a trois semaines, j'............ décidé d'essayer de retrouver mes anciennes camarades de classe.

   h   Toute la famille .... rentrée en France, en 1962.

   i   Mon fils et ma belle-fille .... venus habiter en Lorraine, l'année dernière.

   j   Dans les années 50, nous .... allés vivre en Algérie avec nos enfants.

écrire (pp **écrit**) *to write*	**la petite-fille** *granddaughter*
se marier *to get married*	**la guerre** *war*
le facteur *postman*	**ancien** *old, former*
la belle-fille *daughter-in-law*	

2   Reveal Edith Moreau's life story by putting events a–j (above) into date order, starting with e. Then write a summary in English.

3 Read about the French spa town of Vittel and fit the phrases from the box into the text.

> **le thermalisme** *treatment using spring mineral water*
> **les thermes** *the thermal baths*
> **station thermale** *health spa town*
> **des propriétés curatives** *(from the) healing properties*

Edith Moreau habite à Vittel, ... dans la plaine des Vosges, en Lorraine. En 1854, on y a découvert une source d'eau minérale et on a fondé .... de Vittel. .... devient de plus en plus populaire en France et de nombreux visiteurs viennent à Vittel pour profiter .... de l'eau.

Venir *to come*, which uses **être** in the perfect tense, is irregular in the present tense:

je viens	nous venons
tu viens	vous venez
il/elle/on vient	ils/elles viennent

Devenir *to become* and **revenir** *to come back*, follow the same pattern: **je deviens, je reviens.**

G14

4 Read these replies to a market-research survey in Vittel and work out what they mean, using the glossary only if you get stuck.

Pourquoi est-ce que vous êtes venu(e) à Vittel?
- Je suis venue pour profiter de l'hydrothérapie, du sauna et des cours d'aquagym.
- Pour des raisons de santé: je souffre de rhumatismes et les applications de boue m'aident beaucoup.
- Ma femme et moi, on vient à Vittel tous les ans pour retrouver la santé et la vitalité.
- Je suis venue pour perdre quelques kilos et pour me remettre en forme.
- Nous sommes venus pour profiter des bienfaits de l'eau minérale naturelle.

5 2•37 Now listen to the survey and tick the reasons as you hear them. Note in English the sixth reason you hear, which isn't listed above.

6 Read these adverts for various alternative and complementary health practitioners.

Relaxation et thérapie énergétique manuelle
selon la tradition chinoise

Pour:
- tous problèmes d'ordre **psychique** (stress, dépression, manque de confiance)
- tous problèmes d'ordre **physique** (mal de dos, fatigue, excès de poids)

Entraîneur sportif personnel

à domicile: remise en forme, musculation, perte/prise de poids, traitement efficace de la cellulite.

Douleurs, stress, angoisses, troubles du sommeil, insomnies?
Massage japonais shiatsu
à domicile.

Massage de bien-être
Pour une relaxation profonde et bienfaisante

Avec un praticien certifié en hypnose, vous allez atteindre rapidement et durablement vos objectifs: maigrir, arrêter de fumer, conquérir vos phobies, allergies, angoisses, timidité.

Centre de
chiropraxie
Soins pour toute la famille.
Femmes enceintes.
Athlètes (technique specialisée).
Personnes âgées.
Nous sommes diplômés en chiropraxie infantile.

Vous êtes fatigué? Vous êtes stressé?
Massage aux huiles essentielles
Pour soulager le stress et les maux liés au stress: mal de dos, épaules douloureuses, nervosité, angoisses, etc.

Without using the glossary at first, find the French for these words and phrases: hypnosis, stressed, to slim, painful shoulders, tiredness, well-being, in your own home, beneficial, personal trainer, chiropractic, bodybuilding, pregnant.

The **se** of reflexive infinitives changes to agree with the subject:

Je vais __me__ baigner *I'm going to go swimming*

Elle va __se__ reposer. *She's going to relax.*

Nous allons __nous__ promener. *We're going to go for a walk.*

Ils vont __se__ lever tôt. *They're going to get up early.*

7 Fabienne Joly has just arrived in Vittel and sends a postcard to her friend Noémie, telling her what she's going to do there. Use the items in her suitcase as clues to help you complete her postcard.

> Salut, Noémie!
> Je viens d'arriver* à Vittel: je vais passer une semaine ici. J'ai été très stressée au travail récemment, alors je vais me reposer. Je vais ...
>
> Bisous
> Fabienne   * **Je viens d'arriver** *I have just arrived*

bronzer *to sunbathe*
se baigner *to swim, bathe*
un roman *a novel*

8 At the end of the week, Fabienne writes to her mother, saying she's done all she things she mentioned to Noémie. Finish her postcard.

> Chère maman!
> J'ai passé une très bonne semaine à Vittel.
> Je me suis reposée, je ...
>
> À bientôt
> Fabienne

C'est génial comme idée!

making suggestions

sending and replying to an invitation

saying what people are like

... and what they look like

En France ...

the French love to celebrate an event, and excuses to do so include **anniversaire** *birthday*, **anniversaire de mariage** *wedding anniversary*, **naissance** *birth*, **Saint-Valentin**, **Fête des mères**, **Fête des pères** and even **Fête du beaujolais** for the new Beaujolais wine in November. On such occasions you'll hear **meilleurs vœux!** *best wishes!*, **félicitations!** *congratulations!* and expressions using **bon** or **bonne**: **bon anniversaire**, **bonne fête**.

Reply to an invitation with a simple **Oui, merci** or **Je suis désolé(e)** *I'm sorry*, or something more formal like **J'accepte avec plaisir** or **Je suis malheureusement obligé de refuser**, or even a **SMS** *text message* saying **mr6** *merci*, **DSL** *desolé*.

Making suggestions

1 2•38 Listen to the key language:

On pourrait ...	We could ...
J'ai envie de ...	I'd like to ...
Tu as envie de ...?	Do you fancy ...?
Pourquoi ne pas ...?	Why not ...?
Moi, je propose ...	I suggest ...
C'est génial comme idée!	That's a great idea!

2 Hugo, Juliette and Adrien are brainstorming ideas for their friend Charlotte's 30th birthday. She can't invite people home and doesn't know what to do. First read their suggestions, using the glossary to help.

a **On pourrait aller dîner dans un bon restaurant.**

b **Un apéritif dans un bar en ville, peut-être?**

c **J'ai envie d'aller au nouveau restaurant italien.**

d **On pourrait aller au théâtre.**

e **Moi, je propose un pique-nique.**

f **On pourrait faire un barbecue, chez moi.**

g **Pourquoi ne pas organiser une fête, chez moi?**

3 2•39 Before listening, try to guess which reply is made to each suggestion above. Then listen to check and to find out what they agree on.

1 **Il y a toujours trop de bruit dans les bars.**

2 **On m'a dit qu'on n'y mange pas bien.**

3 **Non, j'ai regardé la météo: il va faire froid ce week-end**

4 **C'est vrai que tu as une jolie terrasse, mais il va faire froid.**

5 **J'ai déjà essayé, il ne reste plus de billets.**

6 **Non, c'est trop cher.**

7 **Ben, oui! C'est génial comme idée!**

En français

You can use **avoir envie de** to say you'd like to do or you feel like doing something. It's followed by an infinitive: **tu as envie de voir un film?**

It's one of several useful phrases based on **avoir**. Others include: **avoir faim** *to be hungry*, **avoir soif** *to be thirsty*, **avoir peur** *to be afraid*, **avoir besoin de** *to need*.

G16

Sending and replying to an invitation

1 Juliette sends an e-mail to invite their friends for Charlotte's birthday. Read it and find out when the party is and what two things Juliette is asking everyone to do.

Salut!
Vous êtes tous invités chez moi, samedi prochain, 27 mai, à 20h00 pour fêter les 30 ans de Charlotte. Apportez chacun un plat pour le buffet!
RSVP avant jeudi, en indiquant quel plat vous pensez apporter.
Merci d'avance et à bientôt.
Juliette

---

2 **2•40** Listen to the key language:

Je veux bien venir.	I'd really like to come.
Avec plaisir/Volontiers.	With pleasure.
Désolé(e), je ne peux pas.	I'm sorry, I can't.
C'est dommage, mais …	It's a pity, but …
J'ai (déjà) quelque chose de prévu.	I've (already) got something planned.

3 **2•41** Adrien's job is to phone Fatima, André and Céline. Listen and choose the answer given by each of them.

Désolée, je ne peux pas. C'est dommage.

Volontiers.

Oui, avec plaisir. Je veux bien.

4 **2•42** Listen to a phone message from Ibrahim. Why can't he come to the party?

Saying what people are like

1   2•43 Listen to the key language:

Tu connais Vanessa?	Do you know Vanessa?
Je ne la connais pas très bien.	I don't know her very well.
Elle est plutôt désagréable.	She's (rather) unpleasant.
Il est super sympa.	He's really nice.
Je ne sais pas.	I don't know.
Elle ne sait pas encore si ...	She doesn't know yet if...

En français

There are two words for *to know* and both are irregular verbs:

● **connaître** to know a person, to be familiar with a thing/place:

Tu connais Ayméric? Do you know Ayméric?

Je le connais bien. I know him well.

● **savoir** to know a fact or how to do something:

Tu sais où il habite? Do you know where he lives?

Je sais faire un excellent gâteau au chocolat. I know how to make a great chocolate cake.

G14

2   2•44 Listen to Adrien and Juliette talking about Vanessa, then fill the gaps in their conversation with **sait**, **sais**, or **si** *if*.

● **Est-ce que Vanessa vient à la fête?**

◆ **Je ne .... pas.**

● **Mais elle t'a téléphoné, non?**

◆ **Oui, mais elle ne .... pas encore .... elle peut venir.**

3   2•45 Adrien is disappointed to get **un SMS** from Vanessa saying **viens pas sam, DSL** *not coming Sat, sorry*. Juliette talks to Charlotte about him. Look at the adjectives below, then listen and write A next to any you hear used to describe Adrien and V next to those used for Vanessa.

poli(e) *polite*	**mignon(ne)** *sweet*
déçu(e) *disappointed*	**drôle** *funny/amusing*
snob *snobbish*	**gentil(le)** *kind/nice*
sympa *nice*	**pas aimable** *not nice*
désagréable *unpleasant*	

... and what they look like

4 **2•46** Listen to the key language

C'est qui?	Who's he/she/that?
Il/Elle est comment?	What's he/she like?
Elle est mince/grosse.	She's slim/fat.
Elle est brune/blonde.	She's dark-haired/fair-haired.
Il fait un mètre quatre-vingts.	He's 1.80m tall.

5 **2•47** Juliette's doing some subtle matchmaking by talking to Adrien about Alice, one of Charlotte's colleagues. Listen and decide whether Alice is:

dark   blonde   slim   chubby

How tall is she?

Si has three meanings: *if, so* and also *yes* when you need a word stronger than **oui** to contradict someone:

Je ne connais pas ta collègue. Si, tu la connais! *I don't know your colleague. Yes, you <u>do</u> know her!*

Tu ne veux pas venir ce soir? Si, je veux bien! *Don't you want to come tonight? Yes, I do!*

En français

---

6 **2•48** Listen as Juliette carries on chatting to Adrien and see if you can spot what Alice's hair is like. In French, **les cheveux** *hair* is plural so you'll hear **ils sont**.

raides *straight*   **frisés** *curly*   **longs** *long*   **courts** *short*

and whether her eyes are:

bleus *blue*   **bruns** *brown*   **verts** *green*   **noisette** *hazel*

7 **2•49** Later Charlotte asks Juliette whether Karim has replied: **Karim a répondu?** Listen, then say in English what he looks like. New phrases to look out for are:

il n'est ni maigre ni gros *he's neither thin nor fat*
chauve *bald*

put it all together

1   Say what these words mean and give their opposites.

mince	court	raide	sérieux
blond	désagréable	impoli	

2   Make these suggestions in French, using the prompts.

a We could have a picnic. (**on pourrait**).

b I'd like to go to the cinema. (**avoir envie de**)

c Do you fancy going to a restaurant? (**avoir envie de**)

d We could organise a party for Camille's birthday. (**on pourrait**)

e Why not go to Versailles tomorrow? (**pourquoi ne pas**)

f Why not have a barbecue? (**pourquoi ne pas**)

3   Fill the gaps with the words in the box.

répondez   organisé   invite   va   fêter

Chers Julien et Cécile
On vous .... à une fête, le
18 juillet, pour .... notre 25ᵉ anniversaire de
mariage. On a .... un dîner au restaurant
Palais du Kashmir, rue Daguerre, à 20h30, et
ensuite on .... rentrer chez nous pour des
cocktails.
.... avant la fin juin, s'il vous plaît.
Amitiés, Isabelle et Jean-Claude

4   Write a similar invitation to a friend, Patrick, for your birthday party on Friday November 16. Tell him you've organised a dinner at **la Brasserie L'Auvergne** at 8pm. Ask him to reply by the end of October. Use the **je** form of the verbs.

5   How would Patrick reply ...

a thanking you, saying it's a lovely idea, he'd love to come;

b apologising, saying it's a pity, he can't come, he's going on holiday?

1 **2•50** Your friend Frédéric phones to invite you to his birthday party.

- **Bonsoir. Je te téléphone pour t'inviter à une soirée pour fêter mon anniversaire.**
- ◆ Say great, with pleasure: when is it?
- **Eh bien, j'ai réservé une table au bistro Romain, pour dix-neuf heures trente jeudi soir.**
- ◆ Say you're sorry, you can't on Thursday: you're going to Strasbourg.
- **Ah, c'est dommage. On pourrait aller boire un pot** (have a drink) **la semaine prochaine – lundi, peut-être?**
- ◆ Say 'what a good idea', you'd like to. You're free on Monday. Wish him a happy birthday and sign off with 'till Monday'.

2 **2•51** A colleague's telling you about Myriam – but you've absolutely no idea who she's talking about.

- **Tu sais, Myriam a trouvé un nouveau travail.**
- ◆ Say you don't know Myriam.
- **Si, tu la connais! Elle est graphiste; elle travaille avec Christine.**
- ◆ Ask what she's like – is she tall?
- **Ben, elle n'est ni grande ni petite. Elle fait à peu près un mètre soixante. Elle a les cheveux longs et raides.**
- ◆ Ask if she's dark-haired. Slim?
- **Brune, oui, et elle est très mince, plutôt maigre.**
- ◆ You've realised who she is. Say yes, you know Myriam: she's really nice.
- **Sympa? Myriam? Je ne pense pas. Moi, je la trouve désagréable!**

3 **2•52 Il est comment, Sébastien?** Describe Sébastien, who's good-looking, slim, he's got dark hair, is 1.80m tall, and really nice, kind and funny.

quiz

1 Which is the odd one out: **raides**, **frisés**, **chauves**, **courts**?
2 If you receive a text message saying **DSL**, what does it mean?
3 How would you say to a group of friends *We could go to the new French restaurant*?
4 Is the missing word **qui** or **que**: **La fille** ...... **vient à la fête**?
5 What can **anniversaire** mean as well as *anniversary*?
6 Would you use **oui** or **si** to mean *yes* here? **Il n'est pas très grand. Mais** ......, **il fait presque deux mètres!**
7 Would you use **je ne sais pas** or **je ne connais pas** to say you don't know who's coming tonight?
8 How would you say *It's a pity, but I've got something planned*?

Now check whether you can ...

- make a suggestion
- send an invitation
- accept an invitation
- refuse politely, apologising and giving a reason
- describe somebody's appearance
- describe somebody's character

Put your learning into practice by seeing if you can describe someone, be it your nearest and dearest or someone from a magazine.

Double the impact of what you've just learnt by putting **très**, **un peu**, **plutôt**, **assez** or, more colloquially, **super** before an adjective.

Try comparing people, using **plus** and **moins**: **Justine est plus petite que Myriam** *Justine's shorter than Myriam*. And if you want to say that someone's *the most* ..., just add the definite article **le/la/les** before **plus** and **moins**: **C'est Laure la plus gentille** *Laure is the nicest*; **Le plus drôle, c'est Karim** *Karim's the most amusing*.

Cuit à la perfection!

following a recipe

choosing wine to complement a dish

commenting on a meal

expressing your appreciation

En France ...

look out for **cuisine du terroir** and **produits du terroir** *regional cooking*
and *regional products*. The names of some dishes reflect their region of
origin: **bœuf bourguignon** translates as beef from Burgundy, and anything
called **à la lyonnaise**, describing dishes cooked with onions, means literally
in the Lyon style. Normandy is famed for its apples and apple products,
such as dishes **au cidre** *cooked in cider*, as well as the apple-based liqueur
Calvados. Many Provençal dishes, including **salade niçoise**, the thick sauce
tapenade and the pizza-like **pissaladière**, contain the succulent local black
olives. For a top-quality wine to complement any dish, choose a bottle
labelled **Appellation d'Origine Contrôlée**.

Following a recipe

un plat à gratin

une gousse d'ail

une casserole

1   Read these verbs that are often found in recipes:

ajouter *to add*	**mettre** *to put*
verser *to pour*	**remuer** *to mix/stir*
couper *to cut*	**écraser** *to crush*
éplucher *to peel*	**(laisser) cuire** *to cook*
saler *to add salt*	**poivrer** *to add pepper*
baisser le feu *to lower the heat*	
retirer du feu *to remove from the heat*	
porter à ébullition *to bring to boiling point*	

2   2•53 Hugo is going to cook **un gratin dauphinois** for Charlotte's birthday. Adrien asks for the recipe, **la recette**. Listen, then fill the gaps in this summary. The summary is more formal and so gives instructions using infinitives, whereas Hugo says what he does and uses **je**.

1   Laver, ... et couper les pommes de terre en tranches très fines.
2   Les .... dans une casserole avec un demi-litre de lait, un peu de beurre et une bonne pincée de noix de muscade. Saler et ....
3   Porter à ébullition, puis .... le feu.
4   .... de temps en temps, pendant cinq minutes.
5   Ajouter 250g de crème fraîche et laisser .... à feu doux, pendant environ cinq minutes, en remuant doucement de temps en temps.
6   Retirer du feu, ... deux gousses d'ail écrasées.
7   .... dans un plat à gratin.
8   Cuire au four à .... pendant .... minutes.

3   2•53 Listen again to Hugo; the complete transcript is on page 127.

Choosing wine to complement a dish

1   **2•54** Listen to the key language:

Il sera …	It will be …
… excellent/parfait avec …	… excellent/perfect with …
Le Bourgogne ira bien avec …	The Burgundy will go well with …
Tout le monde aimera …	Everyone will like …
Il doit être servi …	It should be served …
… chambré/bien frais	… at room temperature/well chilled

2   These are some of the dishes that people have promised to bring to the **fête**. Check the meaning of any new words and sort them into **entrées** *starters*, **plats principaux** *main courses* and **desserts**.

salade de fruits

terrine de thon aux épinards

fricassée de saumon

salade de tomates au basilic

bœuf bourguignon

tarte au citron

gâteau au chocolat et aux amandes

fonds d'artichauts farcis

poulet à l'estragon

3   **2•55** The day before the party, Charlotte tells Hugo about the wine she's bought. Use the glossary to check the words on the left, then listen and say which words describe each of the wines on the right.

blanc	rouge	sec
acidulé	délicat	fruité
léger	robuste	moelleux

Côtes du Rhône
Bourgogne
Chablis
Sancerre

En français

The future tense – which corresponds to the English *will do* – is generally formed by adding a set of endings to the infinitive:
aimer *to like*: j'aimer**ai**, tu aimer**as**, il/elle aimer**a**.

Several common verbs are irregular:

j'irai, tu iras	*I/you will go* (from **aller**)
je serai, tu seras	*I/you will be* (from **être**)
j'aurai, tu auras	*I/you will have* (from **avoir**)
je verrai, tu verras	*I/you will see* (from **voir**)

G18

Commenting on a meal

1 **2•56** Listen to the key language.

Délicieux/Délicieuse!	Delicious!
Parfait(e)! Cuit à la perfection.	Perfect! Cooked to perfection.
pas trop sucré	not too sweet
à mon goût	for my taste
J'ai une passion pour ...	I'm just mad about ...
Ça me rappelle ...	It reminds me of ...

2 **2•57** Before you listen to snatches of conversation heard during the **fête**, see if you can match the two halves of each one.

a Tu as goûté le bœuf bourguignon?	**1** Mmm ... parfait! Cuit à la perfection.
b Tu bois quel vin?	**2** Oui, mais il est fruité et moelleux.
c Il est robuste, ce vin, non?	**3** Délicieuse, acidulée juste comme il faut!
d Tu as aimé le saumon?	**4** Celui-là – je te le conseille. Il est très léger.
e Tu veux un morceau de gâteau?	**5** Oui, il est délicieux. J'aime bien les viandes au vin rouge.
f Qu'est-ce que tu penses de la tarte au citron?	**6** Non, merci, il est un peu trop sucré à mon goût.

3 **2•58** Listen to Adrien asking Alice about the **tarte au citron**. Note who used to make one like it and when. You'll hear **je mangeais** *I used to eat*, **j'étais** *I was* and **on allait** *we used to go*.

Qui? ....   **Quand?** ....

The verbs above ending -ais and -ait convey the English *used to* or *was/were*. This is called the imperfect tense.

je mange *I eat*	je mangeais *I was eating/used to eat*
je suis *I am*	j'étais *I was/used to be*
on va *we go*	on allait *we were going/used to go*
il fait chaud *it's hot*	il faisait chaud *it was hot* **G20**

Expressing your appreciation

1 **2•59** Listen to the key language.

Merci à tous d'être venus.	Thank you all for coming.
Je suis très heureux/euse de vous voir.	I'm very happy to see you.
J'espère que …	I hope (that) …
J'ai passé une super soirée.	I've had a great evening.
Je te souhaite …	I wish you …
… beaucoup de bonheur	… a lot of happiness

2 **2•60** At the end of the meal Charlotte thanks the guests for coming and Juliette wishes her well. Listen and say which of the following Juliette <u>doesn't</u> mention in her toast:

- prosperity
- happiness this year
- a happy birthday
- happiness in years to come

3 Next day, Charlotte writes an e-mail to her three friends to thank them for organising the party. What two things about the party does she particularly mention? What does she thank each individual for?

Chers amis,

Merci beaucoup de votre gentillesse. Vous m'avez fait un très beau cadeau d'anniversaire!

C'était si sympa de retrouver tous mes amis comme ça. Tous les plats étaient délicieux. Hugo, ton gratin dauphinois, je n'en ai jamais goûté d'aussi bon! Adrien, merci d'avoir contacté tous nos amis, tu as eu beaucoup de travail. Et Juliette, merci d'avoir prêté ton appartement, je te suis vraiment reconnaissante.

Je vais passer quelques jours chez mes parents; je vous reverrai la semaine prochaine.

À bientôt!

Charlotte

put it all together

1   Match the verbs on the left with the phrases on the right.

a éplucher	1 une gousse d'ail
b couper	2 le lait dans une casserole
c écraser	3 à ébullition
d porter	4 en tranches fines
e verser	5 les pommes de terre

2   Rearrange these instructions for a soufflé recipe. Start with c.

a Ajouter les jaunes d'œufs.
b Verser la préparation dans un plat à soufflé.
c Chauffer le beurre dans une casserole, y ajouter la farine, laisser cuire une ou deux minutes.
d Ajouter le lait froid d'un seul coup, saler et poivrer.
e Remuer sur le feu jusqu'au premier bouillon.
f Laisser cuire vingt minutes dans un four modéré.
g Battre les blancs en neige ferme. Les ajouter dans la casserole.
h Retirer du feu.
i Remuer vigoureusement.

> **le jaune d'œuf** *egg yolk*   **le blanc d'œuf** *egg white*
> **plat à soufflé** *soufflé dish*   **au premier bouillon** *when it begins to boil*

3   Tick which tense these verbs are in. What do they mean?

		imperfect	present	future
a	je serai			
b	je réponds			
c	j'allais			
d	je fais			
e	j'étais			
f	je mangerai			
g	j'espère			
h	je vois			
i	j'aurai			
j	je travaillais			

1 **2•61** Your neighbours at your holiday home in France invite you to a party. Take part in the general chatter.

You're on **tu** terms with them.

- **Tu aimes le gratin dauphinois?**
- ◆ Say it's delicious – cooked to perfection.
- **Oui, je suis d'accord avec toi. Il est très bon.**
- ◆ Ask if he's tasted the salade niçoise.
- **Non, je n'aime pas tellement les olives: je vais prendre de la salade de tomates. Et le vin? Qu'est-ce que tu penses du Bourgogne?**
- ◆ Comment that it's very good, it's robust and very fruity. Say you like it.

2 **2•62** During the party, you go to talk to your neighbour's grandmother.

- As she's done much of the cooking, say what a lovely-looking (**joli**) cake.
- ◆ **C'est moi qui l'ai fait. C'est une recette de ma mère. Il contient des amandes. J'espère que vous n'êtes pas allergique aux fruits secs. (fruits secs** *nuts/dried fruit*)
- Work out how to say you're not allergic to nuts.
- ◆ **Qu'est-ce que vous pensez de mon gâteau?**
- You taste a piece, say it's delicious. Ask if you can have the recipe.
- ◆ **Oui, bien sûr, je vous la donnerai demain.**
- It's time to go. Thank your neighbour, Claude, say you've enjoyed yourself, the cake was very good, and say goodbye.

quiz

1 What's the French for *a recipe*?
2 What's the main ingredient of **gratin dauphinois**? What would you cook and serve it in?
3 Is *to peel* **éplucher** or **écraser**?
4 **La fête sera géniale!** – does that mean the party <u>was</u> great, <u>is</u> great or <u>will be</u> great?
5 Which is the odd one out? **léger**, **bonheur**, **robuste**, **moelleux**, **fruité**?
6 Does **j'avais** or **j'aurai** mean *I used to have*?
7 If a recipe has the words **à la lyonnaise** in it, what vegetable does it contain?
8 Where would you expect to see the instruction **servir chambré**?

Now check whether you can ...

- understand some of the key words used in recipes
- choose a French wine to complement certain foods
- comment on a meal, giving praise or saying what you're not fond of
- say you're allergic to something
- thank your host and express your appreciation
- recognise the verb endings that mean *will* and *was/were/used to*

If you're interested in French cuisine, there are hundreds of websites devoted to recipes that will give you clear instructions, often with illustrations, and advice on which wine to serve with the dishes, as well as **avis des lecteurs** *the opinions of other readers*. Try putting **recette** and **saumon**, **poulet**, **salade** or other food items into a search engine – you'll get thousands of hits.

En plus 5

Le cœur de l'Europe vous attend!

L'Alsace est située au cœur de l'Europe occidentale, au croisement de la France, la Suisse et l'Allemagne. Le Parlement Européen, le Conseil de l'Europe, la Cour Européenne des Droits de l'Homme et d'autres organismes ont leur siège à Strasbourg.

Cette région a une histoire mouvementée: elle a changé d'identité quatre fois en 80 ans, jusqu'à la fin de la deuxième Guerre Mondiale. Aujourd'hui, ses habitants sont à la fois français et européens: ils vont facilement en Allemagne ou en Suisse pour leur travail, leurs courses ou leurs sorties du week-end.

Allez visiter l'Alsace: vous découvrirez les paysages spectaculaires des Vosges, de magnifiques forêts, les grandes villes culturelles de Strasbourg, Mulhouse et Colmar et une multitude de villages pittoresques.

Le climat alsacien est semi-continental: les hivers y sont rigoureux et les étés très chauds. Colmar est la ville la plus sèche de France: les Vosges la protègent de la pluie. Elle a donc le climat parfait pour la viticulture. La région produit des vins blancs de qualité. Suivez la Route du Vin et achetez quelques bouteilles des célèbres « blancs d'Alsace »: vous ne le regretterez pas! La cuisine alsacienne est réputée dans le monde entier. La spécialité de la région est la choucroute, mais l'Alsace est aussi connue pour sa charcuterie et ses délicieux gâteaux: le streussel, le kougelhopf et la tarte aux myrtilles.

1 **Vrai ou faux? Corrigez les phrases fausses.**

	vrai	faux
a L'Alsace est à côté de la frontière belge.	☐	☐
b La région a toujours fait partie de la France.	☐	☐
c Les Alsaciens n'aiment pas quitter leur pays.	☐	☐
d Il y a de belles plages en Alsace.	☐	☐
e En hiver, il fait très froid.	☐	☐
f Il ne pleut pas beaucoup à Colmar.	☐	☐
g L'Alsace est connue pour ses vins rouges.	☐	☐

There are adjectives relating to regions and towns, for example: **alsacien, midi-pyrénéen, lorrain, breton, provençal, normand, parisien, lyonnais, marseillais, strasbourgeois.** They can also refer to the inhabitants: **les Alsaciens, il est alsacien, elle est alsacienne.**

2 Véronique Garnier est responsable d'un échange dans un institut de formation pour adultes à Colmar. Les partenaires britanniques vont visiter Colmar en avril, et les Français vont chez leurs partenaires britanniques en juin. Le responsable britannique a envoyé à Véronique des renseignements sur les étudiants qui vont participer à l'échange. Lisez ces renseignements et découvrez les paires.

a Armand et Marie-Paule Roux (64 et 62 ans), retraités, habitent dans un appartement au deuxième étage (avec ascenseur), 2 chambres. Pas d'animaux. Aiment le théâtre, l'opéra et l'histoire de l'art.

b Gilles et Ghislaine Bertrand. Gilles (42 ans) est professeur, Ghislaine (44 ans) est médecin. Deux enfants (fils 10 ans et fille 12 ans), aiment beaucoup les animaux, ont un chat et deux lapins. Habitent dans une grande maison ancienne (4 chambres, 2 salles de bains, 3 WC) en banlieue. Aiment faire du vélo et des sports nautiques.

c Philippe et Sally Dumont. Philippe (38 ans) est cuisinier, Sally (37 ans) est née en Irlande, elle est femme au foyer. Habitent un appartement au troisième étage, 3 chambres. Deux filles (8 et 10 ans). Aiment voyager, lire, regarder la télé, écouter de la musique.

1 Edwards family: Tony (engineer, 40), Liz (teacher, 40), Matthew (11) and Jessica (13). Detached house, 4 bedrooms. 2 dogs, 2 guinea pigs. Like skiing, swimming and sailing.

2 Yeoh family: Mark (hotel manager, 41), Angela (receptionist, 39). 2 daughters (9 and 12). Have only just started learning French. Hobbies: watching sport, films, cooking. Mark sings in a folk group.

3 Margaret Rowland, widow aged 67. Lives in a large bungalow, 3 bedrooms and 2 bathrooms. Can't manage stairs, walks with a stick. Interests: literature, the arts, crosswords.

3 **2•63 La famille Edwards est arrivée chez les Bertrand. Écoutez et parlez: dans la conversation, vous êtes Liz.**

- ● Bienvenue en France! Moi, je suis Ghislaine. Mon mari Gilles n'est malheureusement pas encore rentré du travail, mais je vous présente nos enfants, Florian et Lucie.
- ◆ Say you're pleased to meet her and introduce yourself, your husband and children.
- ● Vous avez fait bon voyage?
- ◆ Say yes, you (use **on**) had a good journey. The trains are very quick.
- ● Vous êtes partis de chez vous à quelle heure ce matin?
- ◆ Say you left home at half past six.
- ● Et il faisait quel temps en Angleterre ce matin?
- ◆ Say it was cold.
- ● Vous connaissez l'Alsace?
- ◆ Say you know it a little, you spent a week in Strasbourg alone three years ago.
  Add that last year you all (use **on**) went to the South of France.
  Say you adore France and you've been learning French for three years.

4 **2•64 Quelques jours plus tard, vous parlez avec Gilles.**

- ● Alors, qu'est-ce que vous avez fait aujourd'hui?
- ◆ Say that you (use **on**) went for a walk in the centre of Colmar. You bought some wine and you went to see the Église des Dominicains.
- ● Vous y avez vu le célèbre tableau 'La Vierge au buisson de roses'? *(Madonna of the Roses)*
- ◆ Say yes, you saw it. Unfortunately you haven't any photos because Tony lost his camera. It's a pity.
- ● C'est vrai? Vous avez fait une déclaration de perte?
- ◆ Tell him yes, you went to the police station opposite the tourist office.
- ● J'espère qu'on va le retrouver! En attendant, vous voulez boire un apéritif?
- ◆ Accept with pleasure.

5   As if you were Liz, write a card to a French friend Léa, using your diary as a prompt. Finish by saying you've enjoyed yourself very much, you love Alsace, you're going to come back to France next year!

Mon	Arrived in Alsace, living with a very nice family in a big old house on outskirts of town.
Tue	Sunny weather. Got up early, lots to do here.
Wed	Went to a vineyard in the Vosges. Tasted five different wines, all excellent. Ate sauerkraut in a traditional restaurant.
Thu	Group had a look round (**faire le tour de**) Colmar. What a pretty town! Unfortunately, no photos – Tony lost camera. Reported it at police station. Returned home late. M & Mme B very kind.

Chère Léa,

Amitiés
Liz

Bravo! You've completed *Talk French 2* and should now have a broad enough grasp of the structures of French to cope in everyday situations without being restricted to set phrases.

Don't expect to remember everything you've learnt. Many people find they need to revisit things several times before they really sink in. So go back occasionally, reading and listening to the units again.

The one really important thing to do is to *use* your French. Whenever you can, talk to people and listen to French, read anything you can lay your hands on and write things down.

transcripts and answers

Unit 1

Page 8 Getting to know people

2 ● Comment vous appelez-vous?
  ◆ Je m'appelle **Juliette** Bouchard.
  ● Vous êtes française?
  ◆ Non, je suis suisse. Je suis de Lausanne, en Suisse.
  ● Vous habitez où?
  ◆ J'habite ici, à **Avignon**.
  Her name is Juliette and she lives here in Avignon.

3 ● Bonjour, je **m'appelle** Liam.
  ◆ Enchantée, Liam. On se dit tu?
  ● Oui, d'accord.
  ◆ Tu **es** américain? Anglais?
  ● Je **suis** irlandais. Et toi, comment tu **t'appelles**?
  ◆ Sonia.
  ● **Tu** es d'où?
  ◆ Je suis **de** Saint-Pétersbourg, en Russie. Je **suis** russe. Mais j'habite maintenant **en** Allemagne.
  ● Et moi, j'**habite** en Angleterre, près **de** Cambridge, avec mon frère.

Page 9 Giving information about people

2 ● Je vous présente Sonia. Elle est russe, de Saint-Pétersbourg, en Russie. Elle habite en Allemagne.
  ● Voici Liam. Il est irlandais, mais il habite en Angleterre avec son frère. Ils habitent près de Cambridge.

3 ● Vous êtes mariée?
  ◆ **Oui**. Mon mari s'appelle **François**.
  ● Vous avez des enfants?
  ◆ Oui, on a **trois** enfants – deux fils et une fille. Ils s'appellent Christophe, Pascal et **Aurélie**.
  ● Ils habitent chez vous?

  ◆ Mon fils Christophe est marié et il habite à Genève, en Suisse. Il est médecin. **Pascal et Aurélie** habitent chez nous.
  ● Ils ont quel âge?
  ◆ Eh bien, Christophe a vingt-huit ans, **Pascal a vingt-six ans** et Aurélie a dix-neuf ans.
  a v; b f, son mari s'appelle François (son fils s'appelle Christophe); c f, ils ont trois enfants; d v; e v; f f, Pascal et Aurélie habitent chez leurs parents; g f, son fils Pascal a vingt-six ans.

Page 10 Talking about work

2 ● Qu'est-ce que tu fais comme travail?
  ◆ Je suis médecin. Et toi, qu'est-ce que tu fais comme travail?
  ◆ Je suis plombier.

  ● Qu'est-ce que vous faites comme travail?
  ◆ Je suis rédactrice. Je travaille à la maison. Et vous?
  ● Je suis coiffeur, et le soir, je suis serveur dans un restaurant.
  ● Je suis mécanicien. Je travaille à l'aéroport.
  All the jobs are mentioned except **journaliste** *(journalist).*

3 ● Qu'est-ce que vous faites comme travail, Isabel?
  ◆ Je suis attachée de presse, je travaille pour un grand hôpital depuis **2002**. Et vous, Aldo?
  ● Je suis agent immobilier depuis treize (**13**) ans.

4 Qu'est-ce que vous faites comme travail, Stéphanie? Depuis quand?/ Depuis combien de temps?
  Je suis coiffeuse depuis six ans.

Page 11 Explaining why you're learning French

2 • Sonia, pourquoi est-ce que vous voulez apprendre le français?
  ◆ Parce que j'aime beaucoup les langues.
  • Et vous?
  ◆ Je voudrais travailler en France.
  • Et vous, Lena?
  ◆ Pour aller en Afrique francophone.
  • Et vous, Liam, pourquoi est-ce que vous voulez apprendre le français?
  ◆ Parce que mes amis ont une maison en France.
  • Et vous?
  ◆ Moi, j'adore la France!
  • Et vous, pourquoi est-ce que vous voulez apprendre le français?
  ◆ Pour aider ma fille, qui apprend le français à l'école.
  • Et vous, pourquoi est-ce que vous voulez apprendre le français?
  ◆ Parce que je travaille avec une Française.
  • Et vous?
  ◆ J'adore le pain, le vin et le fromage!
  a 5; b 6; c 7; d 9; e 4; f 1; g 3; h 2; i 8.
  J'aime bien voyager is not mentioned.

3 • Anna, pourquoi voulez-vous apprendre le français?
  ◆ Pour communiquer avec la fiancée de mon fils. Elle est française, elle est de Strasbourg.
  • Et vous apprenez depuis quand?
  ◆ J'apprends le français depuis un an.
  Her son has a French fiancée. She's been learning for one year.

Page 12 Put it all together

1 *a 5; b 6; c 4; d 7; e 1; f 3; g 2.*

2 aimes, aimez, aime
  parle, parle, parlent
  travaillons, travaillent, travailles
  habite, habitent, habitez

3 *a* Je m'appelle Pierre-Yves Berthès. J'ai trente-quatre ans et je suis français. J'habite à Besançon depuis quinze ans; je suis graphiste depuis huit ans.
  b Je vous présente Pierre-Yves Berthès. Il a trente-quatre ans et il est français. Il habite à Besançon depuis quinze ans; il est graphiste depuis huit ans.

Page 13 Now you're talking!

1 • Bonjour. Comment vous appelez-vous?
  ◆ **Je m'appelle Rachel Moore.**
  • Vous êtes américaine?
  ◆ **Non, je suis britannique.**
  • Vous êtes d'où en Grande-Bretagne?
  ◆ **De Bristol.**
  • Qu'est-ce que vous faites comme travail?
  ◆ **Je suis ingénieur chimiste.**
  • Vous êtes ingénieur chimiste depuis combien de temps?
  ◆ **Depuis sept ans.**
  • Pourquoi est-ce que vous voulez apprendre le français?
  ◆ **Parce que j'aime bien voyager et je voudrais travailler en France ou en Suisse.**

2 • **Bonsoir. Comment vous appelez-vous?**
  ◆ Moi, je m'appelle Mathieu – Mathieu Garnier – et voici ma femme Amélie.
  • **Vous habitez où?**
  ◆ On habite à Grenoble.
  • **Vous habitez à Grenoble depuis combien de temps?**
  ◆ Depuis trois ans.
  • **Qu'est-ce que vous faites comme travail?**
  ◆ Moi, je suis graphiste, et Amélie est journaliste. On travaille tous les deux à la maison. C'est pratique parce qu'on a une petite fille.
  • **Elle a quel âge?**
  ◆ Elle a quatorze mois. Elle est adorable!

Page 14 Quiz

1 what kind of work you do;
2 plombier; 3 -e; 4 nous (-ons), vous (-ez); 5 a; 6 depuis; 7 beaucoup; 8 où, pourquoi.

Unit 2

Pages 16 & 17 Using the 24-hour clock and the 12-hour clock

2 ● Il y a trois vols qui partent pour Bordeaux ce soir. Le premier vol part à **seize heures quinze**. Mais il est complet.
   ◆ Et le vol suivant est à quelle heure?
   ● Le vol suivant part à **dix-sept heures trente**. Après ça, il y a un vol à **dix-neuf heures cinquante**.
   ◆ Est-ce qu'il y a un vol avant seize heures?
   ● Non, monsieur.
   Flight times: 16.15, 17.30, 19.50.

3 ● Ici la messagerie de Florent Hubert. Laissez un message après le bip sonore. Merci.
   ◆ Bonjour, Florent. Gustavo à l'appareil. Mon vol arrive à Bordeaux à **dix-huit heures quarante**. *(18.40)*

4 ◆ Florent, excusez-moi pour ce changement, mais **j'arrive à dix-sept heures vingt**. (17.20) À bientôt.

6 *a* 8.45, 9.15, 10.00, 11.00, 12.00, 3.00, 6.00.
   b Bon, Gustavo. Demain, si cela vous convient, nous **partons** de la maison vers neuf heures moins le quart. Nous **arrivons** à l'université vers neuf heures et quart. Le colloque **commence** à dix heures: nous **écoutons** un discours du Ministre de l'Écologie. Après ça, entre onze heures et midi, il y a des présentations: nous avons le choix entre plusieurs sujets. À midi, nous

allons au restaurant, c'est l'heure de déjeuner. Nous sommes libres jusqu'à trois heures. L'après-midi, nous **parlons** de nos recherches. Le colloque finit avant six heures du soir, mais les organisateurs **invitent** tous les délégués à une dégustation à l'École du Vin.

Pages 18 & 19 Talking about your daily routine and the working day

2 *a* Je me réveille à huit heures moins cinq. *(wake up)*
   b Je me lève à sept heures et demie. *(get up)*
   c Je me réveille généralement à huit heures. *(wake up)*
   d Je me réveille à sept heures moins le quart. *(wake up)*
   e Je me lève tard, je me lève à neuf heures moins dix. *(get up)*
   f Je me réveille tôt, vers six heures et demie. *(wake up)*

3 Je me réveille tôt – vers six heures et demie, et je me lève généralement à sept heures moins le quart. Je donne des cours chaque matin, et généralement, l'après-midi, je m'occupe de mes recherches. Après le travail, je rentre chez moi et je me repose. Je dîne en famille vers sept heures. Je me couche vers onze heures.
   He gets up at 6.45; usually does research in the afternoon; goes home and relaxes; about 7pm; about 11pm.

6 ● Nathalie, vous vous levez à quelle heure?
   ◆ Florent et moi, on se réveille tôt, vers six heures et demie. Florent se lève à sept heures moins le quart, et moi, je me lève généralement à huit heures. Je travaille à la maison, je suis webdesigner. Florent travaille à l'université de Bordeaux. Il part de la maison à sept heures vingt-cinq et il prend la voiture.

- Vous travaillez à la maison tous les jours. Alors est-ce que vous faites du sport?
- Oui, c'est essentiel! Généralement, je fais du sport l'après-midi, je vais à la salle de gym ou je vais à la piscine. Le soir, on dîne en famille vers sept heures et on se repose.

a F & N; *b* F; *c* N; *d* N; *e* N; *f* F; *g* F; *h* N; *i* N; *j* F & N.

7 *a* Vous vous levez tôt?
   b Vous travaillez à la maison?
   c Vous faites du sport tous les jours?

Page 20 Put it all together

1 *a* 4; *b* 3; *c* 5; *d* 2; *e* 1.

2 *b* à huit heures du soir; *c* à quatre heures et quart de l'après-midi; *d* à six heures vingt du matin; *e* à onze heures du soir

3 *a* travaille; *b* commence; *c* part; *d* travaille; *e* parlons; *f* me lève; *g* sortez; *h* se lèvent

4 Généralement, je me réveille tôt; je me lève à sept heures et demie; je prends le train; le soir je me repose; je me couche à onze heures/à vingt-trois heures.

Page 21 Now you're talking!

1 ● Steve, vous habitez où?
   ◆ **J'habite à Guildford.**
   ● Mais vous travaillez à Londres, n'est-ce pas?
   ◆ **Oui, je prends le train.**
   ● Vous vous levez généralement à quelle heure?
   ◆ **Je me réveille généralement à six heures et demie et je me lève à sept heures moins dix.**
   ● Et vous partez de la maison à quelle heure?
   ◆ **À sept heures et demie.**
   ● Vous rentrez tard le soir?
   ◆ **Oui, je rentre chez moi à huit heures moins le quart.**

2 ● Bryony, Steve se lève à quelle heure?
   ◆ **Il se lève à sept heures moins dix.**
   ● Il travaille où?
   ◆ **Il travaille à Londres et part de la maison à sept heures et demie.**
   ● Et vous, vous travaillez aussi?
   ◆ **Oui, je travaille de neuf heures du matin à deux heures de l'après-midi.**
   ● Vous aimez faire du sport?
   ◆ **Oui, je vais à la salle de gym tous les jours.**
   ● Le soir, vous dînez ensemble?
   ◆ **Oui, on dîne ensemble à la maison.**
   ● Vous dînez à quelle heure?
   ◆ **On dîne généralement à huit heures du soir.**

Page 22 Quiz

1 3.35pm or twenty-five to four in the afternoon; 15.35 or quinze heures trente-cinq; 2 tôt; 3 global warming; 4 cinquante-deux; 5 se; 6 les recherches; 7 both present tense of aller (to go): je vais (I go), nous allons (we go); 8 evening.

En plus 1
Pages 23–26

2 *a* Luxembourg, Je vais au Luxembourg.
   b Portugal, Je vais au Portugal.
   c Finlande, Je vais en Finlande.
   d Pays-Bas, Je vais aux Pays-Bas.
   e Espagne, Je vais en Espagne.
   f Irlande, Je vais en Irlande.

g Latvia; h Austria; i Poland; j Sweden.

3 *b* Je vous présente Yuki: elle habite à Kobe, au Japon. Elle est employée au guichet de location d'un théâtre depuis treize ans.
   c Je vous présente Chuck: il habite à New York, aux États-Unis. Il est acteur depuis deux mille trois.
   d Je vous présente Rita; elle habite à Toronto, au Canada. Elle est actrice depuis six mois.

e Je vous présente Emily; elle habite à Bradford, au Royaume-Uni. Elle est chanteuse depuis deux mille cinq.

f Je vous présente Vladimir; il habite à Moscou, en Russie. Il est musicien depuis vingt ans.

4 *Gustavo is a student, doing research into climate change in desert zones. Christine suggests going for a walk by the river Garonne.*
Questions: Is this place/seat free? Where are you from? Are you French? Why do you say that? What (job) do you do? Where do you work? What time does the conference end this evening? Would you like to come with me (along the riverside)? Aren't you going to the wine-tasting this evening?

5 travaille; aime; habite; s'appellent; parlons; me lève; commencent; organise; finit; me repose; sors; aime; se couche; attends; pars

6 *Could say:* Salut/Chère Océane, Merci de ta lettre. Ça va bien. Je me lève à dix heures. Je travaille de six heures à onze heures du soir/de dix-huit heures à vingt-trois heures. Je suis serveur dans un café. Je pars en vacances le quinze août, je vais en Italie. À bientôt, Thierry.

Unit 3

Pages 28 & 29 Getting local information and advice

3 ● Bonjour, monsieur, je peux vous aider?
◆ Le musée ouvre à quelle heure?
● Bon, voici **les horaires d'ouverture du musée.**

● Vous avez **un plan de la ville**, s'il vous plaît?
◆ Oui, voilà. Et voici **une carte de la région** aussi.

● Est-ce qu'on peut acheter **un guide des campings**, s'il vous plaît?

◆ Voici un guide des campings de la région, monsieur. C'est gratuit.

● Bonjour, madame, nous cherchons des hôtels pas chers dans la région.
◆ Je peux vous recommander ce **guide des chambres d'hôtes**, et je vous donne aussi **une liste des auberges de jeunesse.**

● Est-ce que vous savez s'il y a un match au stade, cette semaine?
◆ Je ne sais pas, mais on a **un calendrier des événements sportifs**. Attendez, je vais voir.

● Est-ce qu'il y a un bon restaurant près d'ici?
◆ Oui, madame, il y en a beaucoup. Voici **un guide des restaurants**. Le restaurant le plus proche s'appelle L'Ange Gourmand.

● Il faut réserver à l'avance?
◆ Oui, madame. Si vous voulez, je peux appeler le restaurant pour vous.
All the items are mentioned except ***dépliants touristiques*** *and* ***carte routière.***

5 ● Qu'est-ce qu'il y a à **voir** dans la région?
◆ Si vous **aimez** la nature, vous **devez** absolument faire une randonnée: il y a beaucoup de superbes sentiers pour ça dans les environs. Si vous préférez, vous **pouvez** louer un vélo: les pistes cyclables sont très jolies aussi. Si vous **voulez** goûter aux vins de la région, vous **devez** aller visiter un de nos vignobles: il y en a beaucoup par ici. Aux alentours de la ville, il y a un lac où on **peut** faire de la voile ou de la planche à voile. Et puis il y a le château, bien sûr – il **faut** absolument aller le voir.

Page 30 Talking about leisure interests

2 S Dis-moi, Lucas, qu'est-ce que tu fais généralement le week-end?

L En été, je fais de l'escalade.

S Ah bon, et en hiver?

L En hiver, j'aime bien faire du snowboard. C'est ma passion!

S Oh là, c'est dangereux, ça! Et toi, Chantal, tu aimes aussi les sports extrêmes?

C Moi, j'aime les sports nautiques. En été, je fais du ski nautique et de la planche à voile. Je n'aime pas tellement les sports d'hiver.

L Et toi, Sophie, tu es sportive? Tu fais du sport?

S Ben oui, moi, j'aime faire des arts martiaux, surtout le taekwondo. En été, je fais de la randonnée avec ma famille. Ça me plaît beaucoup, j'adore la nature.

Lucas: climbing (summer), snowboarding (winter); Chantal: (summer) water-skiing, surfboarding; Sophie: martial arts especially taekwondo, hiking (summer).

3 Moi, je sors avec mes amis ou avec ma famille, tous les week-ends, on fait des randonnées ou on fait du vélo. On prend généralement de petits sentiers isolés qui sont super. On ne voit personne. J'aime beaucoup la nature. J'aime surtout être à la montagne ... en fait, je ne vais jamais à la mer. À la montagne, il y a des paysages magnifiques et on voit beaucoup d'oiseaux. Si on a de la chance, on voit des aigles. Ça, c'est formidable!

Page 31 Arranging an activity

2 ● Je voudrais faire une randonnée dans la réserve naturelle. Il faut réserver à l'avance?

◆ Non, il ne faut pas réserver. Les randonnées se déroulent tous les jours, à dix heures, et durent environ trois heures et demie. Je vous conseille de porter de bonnes chaussures de marche et d'apporter une gourde d'eau. Je vous conseille

aussi de mettre une crème solaire et un chapeau de soleil.

Not mentioned: You need to take warm clothing.

3 ● Demain on va à la réserve naturelle pour explorer un peu.

◆ Vous y allez comment? À pied ou en voiture? Je te conseille de louer des scooters. Ce n'est pas très cher.

● Y aller en scooter? Géniale comme idée!

He's thinking of going to explore the nature reserve, and perhaps hiring scooters.

4 ● Allô.

◆ Bonjour, madame. Je voudrais louer deux vélos tout terrain. C'est possible?

● Oui, monsieur, c'est pour quand?

◆ Pour demain, de neuf heures à dix-sept heures.

● Oui, bien, pas de problème.

◆ C'est combien la location?

● Alors, un VTT, c'est trois euros de l'heure ou douze euros la journée.

◆ Est-ce qu'il y a un tarif réduit pour les étudiants?

● Non, seulement pour les groupes à partir de dix personnes.

◆ Je peux payer avec une carte de crédit?

● Bien sûr, monsieur. Pas de problème!

From 9am till 5pm; €12 per bike for the day (it's €3 per hour, €12 per day); none (as discounts are only available for groups of ten or more)

Page 32 Put it all together

1 *a de l'; b du; c de la; d des; e du.*

2 *a 5; b 3; c 7; d 1; e 4; f 2; g 6.*

3 I don't have much free time. I like to go out with friends at weekends. We go to town to do some shopping. In summer I go to the beach with my family. It's not far. We play volleyball there. You can go windsurfing there too, but I'm not that keen on water sports.

At home I like listening to music. I never do any sport but I love dancing. I'm mad about it! On Tuesdays I go to a dance class; I'm learning salsa. What do you like doing?

Page 33 Now you're talking!

1 • Bonjour. Je peux vous aider?
   ◆ **Bonjour. Est-ce que vous avez une carte de la région?**
   • Oui, voilà. Et voici une carte routière aussi.
   ◆ **Qu'est-ce qu'il y a à faire dans la région?**
   • Eh bien, il y a beaucoup d'endroits très jolis à visiter. Et le parc du Luberon est tout près. Vous aimez la nature?
   ◆ **Oui. Je voudrais faire une randonnée dans le parc.**
   • Eh bien, oui, c'est possible. Il y a des visites guidées à pied ou à vélo. Voici des renseignements. Les visites sont très populaires: il faut réserver à l'avance.
   ◆ **On peut louer des scooters?**
   • Pas à Roussillon, mais on peut louer des scooters ou des vélos à Gordes.
   ◆ **Merci. Est-ce qu'il y a un bon restaurant à Roussillon?**
   • Oui, si vous aimez la cuisine provençale, je vous conseille le restaurant Le Jardin, juste en face de l'Office du Tourisme.

2 • Qu'est-ce que tu fais le week-end?
   ◆ Je vais en ville, je fais un peu de shopping, et le samedi soir, je sors avec mes amis. On va au cinéma.
   • **Tu fais du sport?**
   ◆ Oui, je fais du vélo et j'aime bien nager aussi.
   • **Tu aimes le foot?**
   ◆ J'adore regarder le foot à la télé. Je suis supporter de l'Olympique de

Marseille. Et toi, qu'est-ce tu aimes faire pendant ton temps libre?

3 *He goes to town, does a bit of shopping, on Saturday evenings goes to the cinema with friends.*

Page 34 Quiz

1 *a road map*; 2 *peut*; 3 *l'escalade*;
4 *Il faut réserver en avance*; 5 *there*;
6 *vélo (bike)*; 7 *faire*; 8 *louer*.

Unit 4

Page 36 Reading property descriptions

1 *a* appartement, chalet, ferme, maison, villa
  b bureau, chambre, cuisine, dressing, salle à manger, salle de bains, salle de billard, salon, séjour, WC
  c barbecue, écurie, garage, piscine, terrasse

Page 37 Describing a property

2a• Bonjour, monsieur, madame. Vous pouvez me décrire votre maison?
   ◆ Nous habitons dans une **ancienne** maison **restaurée** dans un village très **calme,** à dix kilomètres à peu près de la ville. Le village est petit, mais il y a **toutes les facilités à proximité**. Ça nous plaît beaucoup.

b • Bonjour madame, vous habitez un appartement ou une maison?
   ◆ J'habite un appartement duplex.
   • Et il est comment, votre appartement?
   ◆ Eh bien, c'est un appartement qui est assez petit, il est tout **neuf**, et il se trouve **au centre-ville**. C'est très **pratique**. Ce qui me plaît surtout, c'est **le balcon**.

c • Tu peux décrire ta maison?
   ◆ Oui, j'habite avec des amis, **à l'extérieur de la ville**. C'est assez loin de mon travail, mais c'est une jolie maison qui est assez **vieille**.

Elle a **un beau jardin** et **une belle terrasse** où on organise souvent des barbecues.

3 ● Elle est comment, votre maison?
  ◆ Il y a trois chambres et deux salles de bains avec baignoire et douche. Nous avons une grande cuisine bien équipée, où nous mangeons généralement parce qu'il n'y a pas de salle à manger séparée. La pièce principale, c'est le séjour, où il y a une porte-fenêtre qui donne sur la terrasse. La terrasse a une vue magnifique sur les montagnes.
  ● Vous avez aussi un jardin?
  ◆ Oui, nous avons un grand jardin avec des pommiers et des cerisiers.
  Three bedrooms; two bathrooms; kitchen; sitting room; lovely view of the mountains.
  Fruit trees: **pommier** (**pommes** apples) and **cerisier** (**cerises** cherries).

Page 38 Enquiring about a gîte to rent

1 *a* 3 km; *b* 3 bedrooms, 1 bathroom; *c* €460–820; *d* yes – private parking; *e* yes, sheets provided; *f* horse riding, golf, water sports, tennis, fishing and there's a swimming pool; there's also a boules pitch on site.

3 ● Allô, oui?
  ◆ Bonjour, monsieur. Je voudrais louer un gîte en avril et je voudrais savoir si votre gîte est disponible.
  ● Attendez, je vais voir. Eh bien, oui, il est disponible **avant le 22 avril**.
  ◆ Il y a combien de chambres, s'il vous plaît?
  ● Il y en a quatre. Le gîte est pour huit personnes maximum. Tous **les draps sont fournis**, mais **il n'y a pas de serviettes**. Il faut apporter des serviettes.
  ◆ Il y a combien de salles de bains?
  ● **Il y en a deux.**
  ◆ À quel étage?
  ● Au premier étage. Il y a trois WC.

◆ Où se trouve le gîte exactement?
● Il se trouve à trois kilomètres d'Apt, en direction de Bonnieux, dans le Parc National du Luberon. Le gîte est indépendant avec un jardin privé.
◆ On peut garer la voiture?
● **Il n'y a pas de garage**, mais **il y a un emplacement pour garer la voiture**.
◆ Est-ce qu'il y a une machine à laver?
● **Oui**, madame, la cuisine est très bien equipée. **Il y a une machine à laver**, un lave-vaisselle, un micro-ondes, un réfrigérateur et un congélateur.
a f, avant le 22 avril; b f, il y a des draps, il n'y a pas de serviettes; c f, il y a deux salles de bain; d f, il n'y a pas de garage, il y a un emplacement pour garer la voiture; e v.

Page 39 Showing someone round a house

2 ● Entrez, entrez. Voici le séjour: il est **assez** grand, et vous avez la cheminée et la porte-fenêtre qui donne sur la terrasse.
  ◆ **Quel** beau jardin! C'est **quelle** clé pour ouvrir la porte-fenêtre?
  ● C'est la **très** petite clé-là, madame.
  ◆ Merci.
  ● Voici la cuisine. Vous avez le frigo, le congélateur, la machine à laver, le lave-vaisselle, le micro-ondes, le four …
  ◆ Ah oui, elle est **très** bien équipée et **assez** grande.
  ● Au premier étage, il y a les chambres. La troisième est **plutôt** petite, mais la vue de la fenêtre est superbe.
  ◆ C'est **si** joli ici! **Quelle** belle maison!
  ● Alors, voilà. Bon séjour!

3 *a* Maison jumelée avec garage: trois cent vingt-neuf mille euros.
  €329 000

b Appartement tout neuf: quatre cent cinquante-cinq mille euros. *€455 000*

c Maison totalement restaurée: six cent mille euros. *€600 000*

d Villa, six pièces: cinq cent soixante-quinze mille euros. *€575 000*

e Gîte avec piscine: six cent quatre-vingts mille euros. *€680 000*

Page 40 Put it all together

1 jumelé/séparé; loin/près; montagne/mer; ancien/neuf; en plein centre-ville/en banlieue; petit/grand équipé (*equipped*) is left.

2 *a jardin; b salon/séjour; c cuisine; d salle à manger; e WC/salle de bains; f chambre; g terrasse; h garage.*

3 À VENDRE appartement, tout neuf avec vue sur mer, à 5 minutes de la plage. Balcon, 2 chambres, 2 sdb.

À LOUER gîte restauré, calme (mais) à proximité de toutes les facilités. Très joli. Salon, cuisine bien équipée, bureau, 4 chambres, 3 salles de bains. Grand jardin et terrasse.

Page 41 Now you're talking!

1 ◆ Le Rossignol. Allô.
   ● **Je voudrais louer un gîte en Provence. Vous pouvez me décrire Le Rossignol, s'il vous plaît?**
   ◆ Oui, bien sûr. C'est un joli gîte avec terrasse et jardin.
   ● **C'est près de la mer?**
   ◆ Il se trouve à quatre kilomètres environ d'une très belle plage.
   ● **Il y a combien de chambres?**
   ◆ Il y en a trois. Le gîte est pour sept personnes maximum.
   ● **Et il y a combien de salles de bains?**
   ◆ Il y en a une, au premier étage.
   ● **Est-ce qu'il y a une machine à laver?**

◆ Oui, bien sûr.
● **Il y a un lave-vaisselle?**
◆ Non, monsieur, la cuisine est très petite. Elle date de 1894.
● **Bon, merci, au revoir, monsieur.**

2 ● Il est comment, votre gîte?
  ◆ **C'est une ferme restaurée.**
  ● Elle se trouve où?
  ◆ **A cinq kilomètres de Cavalaire.**
  ● Elle est grande, la ferme? Il y a combien de chambres?
  ◆ **Il y en a cinq.**
  ● Ah oui, elle est grande alors!
  ◆ **Oui, et la cuisine est très grande et très bien équipée.**
  ● C'est super! Vous avez un jardin?
  ◆ **Il y a un petit jardin et une belle terrasse.**
  ● Très bien, alors, bon séjour!

Page 42 Quiz

1 sitting room, and stay/holiday; 2 it has been partly restored; 3 vieille; 4 machine à laver; 5 new; 6 Quelle belle plage!; 7 plutôt; 8 disponible à partir du 3 mai.

En plus 2

Pages 43–46

1 *a 3; b 1; c 2.*

2 *a ✗ ✓; b ✓ ✓; c ✓ ✗; d ✓ ✗; e ✗ ✗; f ✓ ✗; g ✓ ✗; h ✓ ✓; i ✓ ✓; j ✓ ✓; k ✓ ✗.*

3 Dear Sir,
I'd like to know if your gîte is available in the first week in September (1st–8th September). There are four of us, my husband, myself and another couple. Could you tell me how much it costs and if we have to pay a deposit? I'd also like to know whether there's a washing machine and a freezer in the kitchen. Thanking you in advance.
Yours sincerely, Eleanor O'Connor.

4 Cher Monsieur,

Je voudrais savoir si votre gîte est disponible pour deux semaines du 18 août au 1ᵉʳ septembre, pour quatre personnes: trois amis et moi-même. Pourriez-vous me dire combien il coûte et si on doit payer des arrhes? Je voudrais aussi savoir s'il y a un lave-vaisselle et un micro-ondes dans la cuisine. Je vous remercie d'avance. Meilleurs sentiments, (*your name*)

6 *1 mes; 2 ton; 3 ses; 4 ta; 5 ma; 6 ton; 7 votre; 8 nos.*

Unit 5

Pages 48 & 49 Shopping for clothes and shoes and bags

2a● Je cherche une chemise blanche, en lin.
  ◆ Vous faites quelle taille, monsieur?
  ● Du quarante-deux.

b ● Je cherche un jean. Taille trente-huit.

c ● Oui, madame?
  ◆ Je voudrais une veste noire.
  ● En coton? En laine? En soie?
  ◆ En soie.

d ● Je cherche un pantalon gris.
  ◆ Vous faites quelle taille, monsieur?
  ● Du quarante-six.

e ● Je cherche un pull vert, en pure laine ou en cachemire, taille moyenne, quarante-deux ou quarante-quatre.

f ● Je peux vous aider?
  ◆ Non merci. Je regarde seulement.
  a white linen shirt, size 42; b pair of jeans, size 38; c black silk jacket; d grey trousers, size 46; e green jumper in pure wool or cashmere, size (medium) 42-44; f just looking.

3 ● Je peux vous aider?
  ◆ Nous cherchons une veste en coton. En bleu ou en blanc.
  ● Quelle taille? C'est pour vous, madame?

  ◆ Non, c'est pour notre fille. Taille trente-six.
  ● Nous avons cette veste bleue en coton.
  ◆ Elle coûte combien?
  ● Cent vingt-cinq euros. J'ai aussi cette veste-ci ...
  a cotton jacket; b blue or white; c their daughter; d €125.

5 ● Je voudrais essayer ces bottes, s'il vous plaît.
  ◆ Vous faites quelle pointure?
  ● Du trente-huit.
  ◆ Je suis désolée, madame, mais je n'ai plus de trente-huit. Je n'ai que du trente-neuf et du quarante. Vous voulez les essayer en noir?
  ● Non, merci. Je les aime en rouge, je n'aime pas le noir. Ah, c'est dommage!
  Size 38; she's offered 39 or 40; black.

6 *a imperméable; b yes (lavable); c fermeture éclair; zippée; une poche.*

7 ● Il y a un problème avec ce sac à dos. Je voudrais l'échanger parce que la fermeture éclair est cassée.
  ◆ Je peux le voir, s'il vous plaît?
  ● Oui, voilà, c'est cette poche à l'intérieure.
  a the zip's broken; b je voudrais l'échanger.

Pages 50 & 51 Expressing your opinion and making comparisons

2 *a la chemise; b la veste; c le pantalon; d le costume*

3 ● Qu'est-ce que tu penses de **ce** costume? Il me va?
  ◆ À mon avis, la veste est un peu trop grande et elle est trop longue. Et puis je n'aime pas la couleur, le noir, c'est trop sombre. Moi, j'aime **celui**-là, le bleu. Mais toi, **lequel** tu préfères?
  ● Moi, j'aime bien **celui**-ci, en gris. Il est classe, et en plus il est

confortable. Le bleu n'est pas très confortable. À ton avis, le pantalon gris n'est pas un peu trop court?
- ◆ Non, il est parfait. Bon, c'est décidé, on prend le gris. Maintenant il faut choisir une chemise. Alors, qu'est-ce que tu penses de **ces** chemises? **Laquelle** tu préfères?
- ● J'aime bien **celle**-ci. Elle fait chic!

5 ◆ Alors, lequel tu préfères? Le bleu ou le vert?
- ● Hmm ... le bleu est plus pratique et il est plus facile à coordonner.
- ◆ Pour moi, le plus beau, c'est le vert, il est plus moulant, plus sexy.
- ● Ben, oui, mais il est trop court, tu ne trouves pas? Il est moins confortable. Je prends le bleu. Il coûte combien? Montre-moi l'étiquette ... Super, il est moins cher que le vert.

Blue: more practical, matches more things, cheaper than the green.
Green: more clingy and sexy, but too short and less comfortable.

6 *b* Le cachemire est plus cher que le coton. Le coton est moins cher que le cachemire.
c Le polyester est plus facile à laver que le cachemire. Le cachemire est moins facile à laver que le polyester.
d Le coton est plus pratique que la soie. La soie est moins pratique que le coton.
e La soie est plus moulante que le coton. Le coton est moins moulant que la soie.

Page 52 Put it all together

1 *a* 4; *b* 1; *c* 3; *d* 2.

2 *a* laquelle; *b* celui; *c* quelle; *d* lequel; *e* celles.

3 *a* Je les prends.
b Yves le cherche.
c On peut la laver à la machine?

d Nous les regardons.
e Est-ce que je peux l'échanger?
f Tu les aimes?

4 ● Je cherche une chemise blanche en coton.
- ● Je cherche un jean, taille trente-huit.
- ● Je cherche une veste bleue, en pure laine, taille quarante.
- ● Je cherche un sac à dos léger.

Page 53 Now you're talking!

1 ● Je peux vous aider?
- ◆ **Je cherche une veste.**
- ● Vous faites quelle taille?
- ◆ **Taille quarante-six.**
- ● Bon, nous avons des vestes en coton, lin, viscose, polyester, jean ... ou peut-être voulez-vous une veste en laine?
- ◆ **Oui, je voudrais une veste en laine.**
- ● De quelle couleur?
- ◆ **Je ne sais pas. En noir ou en gris.**
- ● Nous avons une veste grise en pure laine, ou celle-ci, noire, en laine et cachemire.
- ◆ **Je peux essayer la noire?**
- ● Oui ... Elle vous va très bien. Elle est très élégante.
- ◆ **Elle coûte combien?**
- ● Elle n'est pas très chère – trois cent quatre-vingt-dix euros.

2 ● **Il y a un problème avec ce portefeuille.**
- ◆ Quel problème?
- ● **La fermeture éclair est cassée. Je voudrais l'échanger.**
- ◆ Malheureusement, je n'ai plus de portefeuilles comme ça. Mais j'ai celui-ci. Il vous plaît?
- ● **Hmm ... je ne sais pas. Qu'est-ce que tu penses de celui-ci?**
- ◆ À mon avis, il est un peu trop petit.

3 ● Tu aimes ce pull? Il me va?
- ◆ **À mon avis, il est un peu trop court.**
- ● Tu crois? Moi, je l'aime beaucoup, et il y a une réduction de 25% (vingt-cinq pour cent).

- ◆ **Moi, je préfère celui-ci, et il est moins cher.**
- • Ah oui, il est super, merci!

Page 54 Quiz

1 léger; 2 je cherche, chercher; 3 taille refers to clothes and pointure to shoes; 4 c'est trop cher; 5 cette (veste); 6 que; 7 celui-ci; 8 une fermeture éclair.

Unit 6

Pages 56 & 57 Asking the way and following directions

2 • Excusez-moi, monsieur. Pour aller au commissariat, s'il vous plaît?
- ◆ Le commissariat? Il est dans la rue Ricquet, mais c'est **assez loin**. Vous êtes à pied?
- • Oui.
- ◆ Alors ... comment vous expliquer? Continuez **tout droit jusqu'aux feux**, et puis **tournez à gauche**. Puis vous devez prendre ... la deuxième rue à droite – non, attendez – c'est la troisième rue à droite. Vous continuez **jusqu'au bout de la rue**, c'est une rue assez longue. **Vous traversez un pont, vous passez devant la gare routière** – et le commissariat est **à droite**, non excusez-moi, il est à gauche. Il est **en face d'un collège**.

3 ◆ Vous avez compris?
- • Je crois que oui. Alors, il faut continuer tout droit jusqu'aux feux et puis il faut tourner à **droite**. Puis c'est la troisième rue à droite. On traverse un pont, on passe devant la gare routière, et le commissariat est au bout de la rue, à **droite**.

It should be a left turn (not right) at the traffic lights and the police station is on the left (not right).

4 • Excusez-moi, madame, est-ce qu'il y a un distributeur de billets près d'ici?

- ◆ Oui, il y a une banque dans la rue St-Lazare. Vous devez continuer tout droit en direction du pont de chemin de fer, puis vous devez prendre la première rue à gauche, puis la première rue à droite. La banque se trouve à droite.

You end up at b.

6 • Excusez-moi, monsieur. Le commissariat, c'est bien par ici?
- ◆ Non, vous vous trompez de direction, madame. Il est dans la rue Ricquet, c'est assez loin d'ici. Mais vous pouvez prendre le bus, le numéro soixante-cinq. L'arrêt est ici. Vous devez descendre au troisième arrêt. Ce n'est pas loin, cinq minutes au plus. Le commissariat se trouve tout près de la gare routière.
- • Merci beaucoup, monsieur.

a far; b 65; c 3rd; d 5; e near/ close to the bus station.

Page 58 Explaining what's happened

2 • Bonjour, Colette, c'est moi, Jack.
- ◆ Salut, Jack. Ça va?
- • Non, ça ne va pas très bien. J'ai **perdu** mon ordinateur portable.
- ◆ Comment? Je n'ai pas **entendu**. Qu'est-ce que tu as **dit**?
- • J'ai **perdu** mon ordinateur portable! Enfin, on m'a **volé** mon ordinateur portable!
- ◆ Ah, c'est pas possible! Tu as **fait** une déclaration à la police? Tu dois aller tout de suite au commissariat.
- • Oui, oui, on y va maintenant.
- ◆ Allez, bon courage! À plus tard.

3 • Salut, François, c'est Jack. On est en retard. On a perdu ...
- ◆ On a perdu?
- • Euh, moi, j'ai perdu mon ordinateur portable.

Because it was Jack that lost the laptop, but he's saying that 'we' lost it.

Page 59 Reporting a problem

2 • Eh bien, monsieur, qu'est-ce qui est
      arrivé?
   ◆ J'ai perdu mon ordinateur portable.
      Ce matin, vers onze heures, au café
      en face de la gare, j'ai mis mon
      ordinateur portable par terre, j'ai
      commandé un café au lait, j'ai bu
      mon café et j'ai lu mon journal. À
      peu près quinze minutes plus tard,
      j'ai payé, j'ai mis mon portefeuille
      dans ma poche ... et puis j'ai
      cherché, mais je n'ai pas trouvé
      mon ordinateur.
   • Bon, voyons ... Vous avez vu
      quelqu'un près de votre table?
   ◆ Non, je n'ai vu personne.
   Correct order: f, g, e, a, d, b, c, h.

3 Il a mis son ordinateur portable par
   terre, il a commandé un café au lait,
   il a bu son café, il a lu son journal, il a
   payé, il a mis son portefeuille dans sa
   poche, il a cherché, il n'a pas trouvé
   son ordinateur.

Page 60 Put it all together

1 *a 3; b 4; c 1; d 5; e 2.*

2 *a* J'ai perdu mon passeport.
   b Tu as commandé un café?
   c Vous avez compris le guide?
   d Niamh a réservé une table.
   e Vous avez entendu?
   f Ils/Elles ont fait une déclaration à la
      police.
   g Elle n'a vu personne.
   h Il a visité le musée.

3 j'ai invité Nathalie au restaurant
   j'ai acheté du pain
   j'ai mis le linge dans la machine à
   laver
   je n'ai pas téléphoné à Robert
   je n'ai pas retiré de l'argent.

Page 61 Now you're talking!

1 • **Excusez-moi, monsieur, vous
      pouvez nous aider?**

   ◆ Oui, bien sûr. Vous avez un
      problème?
   • **Pour aller au commissariat, s'il
      vous plaît?**
   ◆ C'est assez loin – rue St-Germain.
      Vous devez prendre l'autobus
      numéro seize.
   • **Excusez-moi, madame, le
      commissariat, c'est bien par ici?**
   ◆ Oui, continuez tout droit, et
      tournez à droite après les feux. Le
      commissariat se trouve à gauche,
      en face d'un supermarché.
   • **Merci, madame.**

2 It's quite far, in rue St-Germain, take
   bus number 16. After the bus, go
   straight on and turn right after the
   lights, and it's on the left, opposite a
   hypermarket.

3 • Allô! Paul Bauchet.
   ◆ **Qu'est-ce qui est arrivé?**
   • J'ai perdu ...
   ◆ **Qu'est-ce que tu as dit?**
   • J'ai perdu mon portefeuille. Je l'ai
      perdu au bureau hier. Tu l'as vu?
   ◆ **Oui, Stéphane a trouvé un
      portefeuille au bureau. Un
      portefeuille noir.**
   • Ah, oui! Ça doit être mon
      portefeuille. Merci. Et vous deux,
      qu'est-ce que vous avez fait
      aujourd'hui?
   ◆ **On a visité le château.**
   • Et vous avez déjeuné où?
   ◆ **On a dejeuné dans un petit
      restaurant au centre-ville.**
   • Très bien!

Page 62 Quiz

*1 17 and 112; 2 la gare, la gare
routière, le commissariat; 3 tout
droit means 'straight on' and à droite
means 'to the right' or 'on the right';
4 whether you have understood;
5 you've got the wrong number;
6 La banque, c'est bien par ici?
7 descendre; 8 j'ai acheté, j'ai vendu.*

En plus 3

1 *Name should be Colette; address should be rue; place of birth Toulon; date of loss Tuesday 20 March; time 20.00; lost at sports centre; handbag; contains €30–35 (cost €120); contains not identity card but credit card and season ticket; one photo not two.*

3 *a f, Sylvie a acheté un débardeur en Espagne; b v; c f, Vincent/Sylvie voudrait changer d'emploi; d v; e f, son chef n'est pas sympa; f f, Sylvie a eu des entretiens/Vincent a un entretien la semaine prochaine; g v.*

4 passé; acheté; eu *(from avoir)*; trouvé; fait; été *(from être)*; vu; oublié; téléphoné; reçu *(from* recevoir).

5 Could say:
Salut Gabi, Merci pour ton e-mail. Moi, je n'ai jamais visité l'Amérique du Sud. J'ai eu trois entretiens. Je préfère le Collège Jeanne d'Arc, il est plus loin que le collège d'Amina mais les autres professeurs sont plus gentils. Je n'ai plus de nouvelles. À bientôt, Sylvie

6 *Vous mangez de la viande?* Jamais! *Qui parle espagnol dans votre société?* Personne.
Tu as vu quelque chose? Non, je n'ai rien vu.
Vous avez acheté deux chemises? Non, je n'ai acheté qu'une chemise.

7 *a* étui; *b* gants; *c* blouson; *d* sac de voyage; *e* ceinture; *f* collier.

Unit 7

Page 68 Talking about your holiday plans

2 ● Tu vas où en vacances cette année?
  ◆ Je vais en Corse avec mes parents.

  ● Et vous, vous allez où en vacances cette année?

  ◆ On va dans le Midi, comme d'habitude.

  ● Excusez-moi, vous allez où en vacances cette année?
  ◆ **Je vais au Pays Basque, dans un petit village qui se trouve près de Biarritz.**

  ● Et vous, vous allez où en vacances cette année?
  ◆ **Nous allons au bord de la mer avec nos enfants.**

  ● Et toi, tu vas où en vacances cette année?
  ◆ **Je vais aller en Bretagne, cet été. Les parents de mon copain ont un gîte à Josselin.**

3 ● Excusez-moi, vous **allez** où en vacances cette année?
  ◆ Je vais **aller** en Provence – toute seule! Je suis divorcée et ma fille **va** en vacances avec son père. Ils **vont** en Martinique.

Page 69 Saying what the weather's like

1 ● Excusez-moi, vous allez où en vacances cette année?
  ◆ Je vais au Pays Basque, dans un petit village qui se trouve près de Biarritz.
  ● Il fait quel temps à Biarritz?
  ◆ Eh bien, en été, en juillet et en août il fait beau temps. Il y a du soleil. Il fait chaud, mais pas trop chaud à cause de la proximité de l'océan. La température moyenne est de **vingt-deux** degrés. C'est un climat humide: il y a assez souvent des averses.
  Fine; sunny; hot but not too hot; humid, often showers. 22°.

Pages 70 & 71 Talking about past holidays and saying what you did

2*a* ● Bonjour, tu es allée où en vacances l'année dernière?

◆ Je suis allée au bord de la mer. *(one female)*

b ● Et vous, monsieur, vous êtes allé où en vacances l'année dernière?
◆ Je suis allé à Biarritz, comme d'habitude. Il a fait chaud. *(one male)*

c ● Bonjour, monsieur, vous êtes allé où en vacances l'année dernière?
◆ Je suis allé sur la côte ouest de l'Irlande. Moi, j'aime la tranquillité. *(one male)*

d ● Excusez-moi, madame, monsieur, vous êtes allés où en vacances, l'année dernière?
◆ L'été dernier, nous sommes allés dans le Midi, à St-Tropez. C'est très joli ... mais très cher. *(more than one)*

e ● Bonjour, tu es allé où en vacances l'année dernière?
◆ Je suis allé en Guadeloupe pour voir mes parents. *(one male)*

f ● Bonjour, monsieur, madame. Vous pouvez me dire ... vous êtes allés où en vacances l'année dernière?
◆ On n'est pas partis en vacances l'année dernière. Nos amis américains sont venus en France, alors on est restés chez nous. Il y a deux ans, on est allés chez eux, en Californie. *(more than one)*

3 Je suis allé en Corse avec ma copine; On est allées en Martinique l'année dernière; Nous sommes allés en Irlande avec des amis; Je suis allée à Paris il y a deux ans.

5 ● Salut, Arnaud, tu as passé un bon week-end?
◆ Oui, super, merci.
● Qu'est-ce que tu as fait? Tu es allé où?
◆ Je suis allé à Bruxelles avec ma copine. Et toi, qu'est-ce que tu as fait?
● Rien, je suis resté chez moi.
He went to Brussels with his girlfriend.

6 ● Alors, qu'est-ce que vous y avez fait?
◆ Comme tu le sais, Bruxelles n'est pas loin du tout. Alors, on est partis de la maison vers sept heures du matin et vers neuf heures et quart on est arrivés à Bruxelles. Avec le TGV, c'est rapide, hein? D'abord on est allés à la Grand-Place, qui est très belle. L'architecture est superbe. Après ça, on est allés à l'Atomium. On est montés dans la sphère la plus haute, où il y a un restaurant. On y a déjeuné, il y a une très belle vue de la ville. On a pris l'ascenseur pour monter – c'est très rapide – mais on est descendus par les escalators, qui se trouvent dans les tubes entre les sphères. C'est une structure très intéressante – je te conseille d'y aller. On est rentrés à Paris vers dix heures du soir.
Correct order: e, b, h, a, f, c, g, d.

Page 72 Put it all together

1 *a* 3; *b* 5; *c* 6; *d* 4; *e* 2; *f* 1.

2 *a* vas; *b* allons; *c* allez; *d* vais; *e* vont; *f* va; *g* va; *h* vais.

3 L'année dernière, je suis allé/allée en vacances en Corse avec des amis. On est partis/parties en bateau de Marseille, et on est arrivés/arrivées à Bastia, en Corse. Il a fait très chaud là-bas. On a fait du ski nautique.

4 *a* Je vais au bord de la mer.
b Nous allons dans le Midi en famille.
c Je vais aller sur la côte ouest de l'Irlande avec des amis.
d On ne part pas en vacances cette année, on reste à la maison/chez nous.

Page 73 Now you're talking!

1 ● Dis-moi: il fait quel temps?
◆ **Il fait beau, il y a du soleil.**
● Il ne fait pas froid?
◆ **Non, il fait vingt-et-un degrés.**

2a ● Tu vas où en vacances cette année?
  ◆ **Je vais en Italie.**
  ● Tu y vas seul(e)?
  ◆ **Non, j'y vais avec des amis.**

b ● Vous allez en France cette année?
  ◆ **Oui, je vais aller en Provence avec mon compagnon/ma compagne.**
  ● C'est une belle région! Vous allez à la montagne ou au bord de la mer?
  ◆ **À la montagne: mon cousin a un gîte près de Gordes.**
  ● Ah, c'est super! C'est un très joli village.

3 ● Vous êtes allé(e) où, l'été dernier?
  ◆ **Je suis allé(e) en Bretagne: j'y suis allé(e) avec des amis.**
  ● Vous y êtes allés en voiture, ou en train?
  ◆ **On y est allés en train.**
  ● Il a fait quel temps?
  ◆ **Il a fait assez chaud, vingt-deux degrés.**

Page 74 Quiz

1 midi and Midi; 2 pont; 3 vas; 4 aller, arriver; 5 il y a dix ans; 6 il fait mauvais (temps); 7 il fait chaud is present, il a fait chaud is perfect tense/ past; 8 je suis tombé/je suis tombée.

Unit 8

Page 76 Saying how you're feeling

2 *Élodie isn't going into work because she's not well.*

3 ● Élodie, tu ne **vas** pas bien?
  ◆ Non, je suis malade. Je ne vais pas **bien** du tout.
  ● Ma pauvre! Qu'est-ce que tu as?
  ◆ J'ai **mal** partout. Je peux à peine marcher.
  ● Quoi! C'est affreux! Tu **as** eu un accident?
  ◆ Non, non. Hier, Michel et moi, on **est** allés à la montagne – on **a** fait cent kilomètres!

● Élodie, n'exagère pas!
  ◆ D'accord, dix kilomètres. Et moi, je **suis** tombée! J'ai eu peur!
  ● Bon, écoute, excuse-moi, mais j'ai une réunion dans cinq minutes. Je suis vraiment désolée. On se retrouve demain?

4 Salut, Sandrine. Élodie ne va pas au travail aujourd'hui. Elle ne va pas bien. Elle est allée à la montagne avec Michel hier, elle est tombée, et elle a mal partout.

Page 77 Relating an incident

2 Hier, Élodie et moi, **on s'est promenés** à la campagne. Je pense qu'**elle s'est bien amusée.** Moi, en tout cas, **je me suis bien amusé**. Je suis monté jusqu'au sommet d'une belle petite colline. **Élodie s'est arrêtée** à mi-chemin et **elle s'est reposée. On s'est retrouvés** plus tard pour descendre. Elle est tombée une fois, mais heur-eusement, **elle ne s'est pas fait** mal.

3 *a* Je me suis arrêté et je me suis reposé.
  b Nous nous sommes bien amusés. On s'est bien amusés.

Page 78 Describing symptoms

1 ● Tu vas mieux?
  ◆ Non. Aïe! J'ai mal aux jambes, j'ai mal au genou – c'est mon genou gauche – et j'ai mal au dos …
  ● Hmm, va voir le médecin, c'est peut-être grave!
  Her legs and (left) knee and back hurt.

2 ● Fabienne, c'est Élodie.
  ◆ Bonjour, Élodie, écoute, je ne peux pas trop parler maintenant. Théo est malade, le pauvre. **Il a mal à la gorge, mal à la tête, mal au ventre et il tousse.** Je vais téléphoner au médecin. Et toi, comment vas-tu?

Page 79 Following instructions

2 ● Je peux à peine marcher. J'ai mal

aux jambes et j'ai mal au genou.

- ◆ Aha. Faites voir? Qu'est-ce que vous avez fait?
- ● Je suis tombée, dimanche, à la montagne.
- ◆ Ça vous fait mal ici?
- ● Non ... euh, peut-être un peu.
- ◆ Vous pouvez plier le genou?
- ● Oui, un peu, mais – aïe! Ça fait mal.
- ◆ Hmm. Ce n'est pas grave. C'est une contusion, un petit bleu, c'est tout. Prenez des analgésiques pendant deux ou trois jours, reposez-vous et faites peu d'exercice.
- ● C'est tout?
- ◆ Oui, oui, ce n'est pas grave. Ne vous inquiétez pas.

3 ● Prenez deux comprimés avec un peu d'eau, quatre fois par jour, pendant deux ou trois jours, après les repas si possible. Ne buvez pas d'alcool et ne dépassez pas la dose prescrite.

Take two tablets, with water, four times a day for two or three days, after meals if possible. Don't drink alcohol and do not exceed the recommended dose.

Page 80 Put it all together

1 bras *(others all facial features)*; tête *(others all parts of the leg)*; pharmacien *(others all doctor)*.

2 *a* 3; *b* 5; *c* 6; *d* 7; *e* 1; *f* 4; *g* 2.

3 Salut, Antoine.
Je suis désolé, mais je ne peux pas aller au cinéma ce soir. Je ne vais pas bien du tout, j'ai de la fièvre, et j'ai mal au dos et mal aux jambes. [*Name*]/mon mari/ma femme/mon compagnon/ma compagne a mal à la tête et mal à la gorge.
Et toi, comment vas-tu? Tu es allé au travail aujourd'hui? Tu as vu Thomas? À bientôt. [*Your name*]

Page 81 Now you're talking!

1 ● **Bonjour, Élodie. Tu vas bien?**

- ◆ Non, je ne vais pas bien du tout.
- ● **Qu'est-ce que tu as?**
- ◆ J'ai mal au dos, j'ai mal au genou. Je peux à peine marcher.
- ● **Ma pauvre! Tu as eu un accident?**
- ◆ Un accident? Mais non! C'est la montagne – hier – tu comprends?
- ● **Mais hier, on s'est promenés à la campagne.**
- ◆ Oui, on a fait vingt kilomètres et je suis tombée, et maintenant j'ai mal partout et je peux à peine marcher.
- ● **On a fait cinq kilomètres. Euh ... excuse-moi, mais j'ai une réunion dans cinq minutes.**

2 ● Comment vas-tu aujourd'hui?
- ◆ **Je ne vais pas bien.**
- ● Désolée. Qu'est-ce que tu as?
- ◆ **J'ai mal à la tête et mal à la gorge.**
- ● Mon pauvre!
- ◆ **Et j'ai mal au dos.**
- ● Tu as de la fièvre?
- ◆ **Oui, et je tousse et j'ai mal à l'oreille.**
- ● À mon avis, tu as la grippe. Tu as pris quelque chose?
- ◆ **Non, mais je voudrais des analgésiques.**
- ● J'en ai qui sont très efficaces. Attends une minute.

Page 82 Quiz

1 *SAMU, 15;* 2 *Qu'est-ce-que tu as?;*
3 *peine;* 4 *she's feeling fine/better;*
5 *j'ai mal au ventre, j'ai mal à la tête;*
6 *eu;* 7 *il s'est fait mal;* 8 *reposez-vous, ne vous inquiétez pas.*

En plus 4

Pages 83–86

1 *a* ai; *b* est; *c* suis; *d* est; *e* suis; *f* a; *g* ai; *h* est; *i* sont; *j* sommes.

2 *Correct order: e, c, j, h, b, d, i, g, a, f. Edith Moreau was born in Vittel in 1930; she got married four years after the end of World War II; in the 1950s*

the family went to live in Algeria; the whole family returned to France in 1962; granddaughter born in Grenoble 1991; husband died three years ago; son and daughter-in-law came to live in Lorraine last year; three weeks ago she decided to search for her old classmates; last week wrote a letter to the local newspaper; yesterday the postman brought two replies.

3 station thermale; les thermes; Le thermalisme; des propriétés curatives

5 ● Pourquoi est-ce que vous êtes venue à Vittel?
  ◆ Je suis venue pour perdre quelques kilos et pour me remettre en forme.

  ● Pourquoi est-ce que vous êtes venus à Vittel?
  ◆ Ma femme et moi, on vient à Vittel tous les ans pour retrouver la santé et la vitalité.

  ● Pourquoi est-ce que vous êtes venue ici?
  ◆ Pour des raisons de santé: je souffre de rhumatismes et les applications de boue m'aident beaucoup.

  ● Pourquoi vous êtes venus à Vittel?
  ◆ Nous sommes venus pour profiter des bienfaits de l'eau minérale naturelle.

  ● Pourquoi êtes-vous venue ici?
  ◆ Je suis venue pour profiter de l'hydrothérapie, du sauna et des cours d'aquagym.

  ● Et vous, pourquoi est-ce que vous êtes venue à Vittel?
  ◆ Ma sœur est venue ici l'année dernière et elle m'a recommandé le calme, la beauté de la région et les cures thermales traditionnelles.
Her sister came last year and recommended the peace and quiet, the beauty of the area and the traditional mineral water treatments.

6 hypnose, stressé, maigrir, épaules douloureuses, fatigue, bien-être, à domicile, bienfaisant(e), entraîneur sportif personnel, chiropraxie, musculation, enceinte(s).

7 Je vais me baigner/nager, je vais bronzer, je vais écrire des lettres, je vais lire quelques livres/romans, je vais jouer au tennis, je vais aller à/ visiter Nancy.

8 Je me suis baignée/j'ai nagé, j'ai bronzé, j'ai écrit des/quelques lettres, j'ai lu quelques livres/romans, je suis allée à Nancy/j'ai visité Nancy/j'ai fait une excursion à Nancy.

Unit 9

Page 88 Making suggestions

3 *H* Tu dois absolument fêter ton anniversaire, Charlotte. On n'a pas trente ans tous les jours!
  C Oui, mais je ne peux pas inviter tout le monde chez moi, c'est trop petit.
  H On pourrait aller dîner dans un bon restaurant.
  A Non, c'est trop cher.
  J Un apéritif dans un bar en ville, peut-être?
  C Non, il y a toujours trop de bruit dans les bars.
  J J'ai envie d'aller au nouveau restaurant italien, en ville.
  H On m'a dit qu'on n'y mange pas bien.
  C On pourrait aller au théâtre voir *Les Misérables*.
  A J'ai déjà essayé, il ne reste plus de billets.
    Moi, je propose un pique-nique.
  C Non, j'ai regardé la météo: il va faire froid ce week-end.
  H On pourrait faire un barbecue chez moi.
  C C'est vrai que tu as une jolie terrasse, mais je t'ai déjà dit qu'il va faire froid!

J Pourquoi ne pas organiser une fête chez moi?

H Ben, oui! C'est génial comme idée!

A Oui, tu as un grand appartement. C'est gentil de ta part.

C Vraiment? Si tu fais ça pour moi, c'est moi qui apporte le vin!

● Ouais! Ben, voilà. On est d'accord! Génial! Super!

a 6; b 1; c 2; d 5; e 3; f 4; g 7.

Page 89 Sending and replying to an invitation

1 *next Saturday, 27th May at 8pm; reply before Thursday, saying whether they can come and what food item they'd like to contribute.*

3 ● Bonjour, Fatima, c'est Adrien.

◆ Salut, Adrien.

● On organise une fête pour Charlotte, ce week-end. C'est son anniversaire, elle va avoir trente ans. Samedi soir, chez Juliette. Tu es libre? Tu peux venir?

◆ **Volontiers**. C'est à quelle heure?

● André, salut, c'est Adrien. Tu sais que c'est l'anniversaire de Charlotte, samedi prochain? On prépare une fête pour elle, samedi soir à vingt heures, chez Juliette. Tu veux venir?

◆ **Oui, avec plaisir, je veux bien.** Merci.

● Bonjour, Céline, c'est Adrien. Tu es libre samedi soir? C'est l'anniversaire de Charlotte et on fait la fête. Tu peux venir?

◆ **Désolée, je ne peux pas. C'est dommage**, mais je vais passer le week-end chez mes parents. Mon père est malade.

4 ● Salut, Adrien, c'est Ibrahim à l'appareil. Je t'appelle juste parce que je ne peux pas venir samedi soir. Je pars en vacances vendredi. Le bonjour à Charlotte de ma part,

s'il te plaît. À bientôt.

Because he's going on holiday on Friday.

Pages 90–91 Saying what people are like and what they look like

2 ● Est-ce que Vanessa vient à la fête?

◆ Je ne **sais** pas.

● Mais elle t'a téléphoné, non?

◆ Oui, mais elle ne **sait** pas encore **si** elle peut venir.

3 ● Tu connais Vanessa?

◆ Oui, bien sûr. Pourquoi?

● Elle ne vient pas à ta fête. Adrien est très déçu.

◆ Il l'aime bien, j'ai l'impression, non?

● Oui. Et je ne vois vraiment pas pourquoi – à mon avis elle n'est pas très aimable.

◆ Mais si, elle est gentille!

● Tu trouves, toi? Ben, pas moi! Je ne la trouve pas sympa: elle est snob, elle est désagréable. Ah là là! Pauvre Adrien! Lui qui est si mignon, si poli, si drôle … il est beaucoup trop sympa pour elle!

◆ Mais dis-donc, Juliette, tu es jalouse, peut-être!

A: déçu, mignon, poli, drôle, (trop) sympa.

V: (pas très) aimable, gentille, (pas) sympa, snob, désagréable.

5 ● J'ai reçu la réponse d'Alice. Elle va venir samedi soir.

◆ C'est qui, Alice?

● C'est une collègue de Charlotte.

◆ Elle est comment, cette Alice? Petite? Blonde?

● Non, elle est grande, mince et brune. Elle fait à peu près un mètre soixante-dix.

◆ Non, je ne la connais pas.

Alice is tall, slim, dark-haired, about 1.70m tall.

6 ● Non, je ne la connais pas.

◆ Si, tu la connais! Elle a les yeux très bleus, les cheveux bruns et courts.

- Elle a les cheveux frisés?
- Non, ils sont raides.
- Hmm … Ah! Oui! Alice! Je vois maintenant … La fille qui sourit beaucoup.
- Oui, c'est elle!

She's got short, straight, dark hair; her eyes are blue.

7
- Karim a répondu?
- C'est qui, Karim? Le petit gros? Chauve?
- Non, il n'est pas chauve. Il a de beaux cheveux bruns frisés. Et il n'est ni maigre ni gros. Il porte souvent un jean et des baskets. Et il n'est pas petit! Il fait presque deux mètres. Il est assez beau, il est sympa, il est très drôle …
- Ah bon? Alors j'espère qu'il va venir!

He's got nice curly brown hair; neither thin nor fat, often wears jeans and trainers; not short – nearly 2m tall, quite good-looking, nice, very funny.

Page 92 Put it all together

1 mince *slim* gros *fat*; court *short* long *long*; raide *straight* frisé *curly*; sérieux *serious* drôle *amusing*; blond *fair-haired* brun *dark-haired*; désagréable *unpleasant* sympa/gentil *nice*; impoli *rude* poli *polite*.

2 a On pourrait faire un pique-nique.
b J'ai envie d'aller au cinéma.
c Tu as/Vous avez envie d'aller au restaurant/d'aller dîner dans un restaurant?
d On pourrait organiser une fête pour l'anniversaire de Camille.
e Pourquoi ne pas aller à Versailles demain?
f Pourquoi ne pas faire un barbecue?

3 invite; fêter; organisé; va; Répondez

4 Cher Patrick, Je t'invite à une fête le vendredi 16 novembre, pour fêter mon anniversaire. J'ai organisé un

dîner à la brasserie L'Auvergne à 20h00. Réponds avant la fin d'octobre, s'il te plaît. Amitiés [*your name*]

5 a Merci. Quelle bonne idée!/C'est une bonne idée. Je veux bien venir.
b Désolé, c'est dommage. Je ne peux pas venir, je pars en vacances.

Page 93 Now you're talking!

1
- Bonsoir. Je te téléphone pour t'inviter à une soirée pour célébrer mon anniversaire.
- **Génial! Volontiers! C'est quand?**
- Eh bien, j'ai réservé une table au bistro Romain, pour dix-neuf heures trente jeudi soir.
- **Désolé(e), je ne peux pas jeudi, je vais à Strasbourg.**
- Ah, c'est dommage. On pourrait aller boire un pot la semaine prochaine – lundi peut-être?
- **Bonne idée, je veux bien. Je suis libre lundi. Alors, bon anniversaire! À lundi!**

2
- Tu sais, Myriam a trouvé un nouveau travail.
- **Je ne connais pas Myriam.**
- Si, tu la connais! Elle est graphiste, elle travaille avec Christine.
- **Elle est comment? Elle est grande?**
- Ben, elle n'est ni grande ni petite. Elle fait à peu près un mètre soixante. Elle a les cheveux longs et raides.
- **Elle est brune? Mince?**
- Brune, oui, et elle est très mince, plutôt maigre.
- **Ah oui, je connais Myriam. Elle est super sympa.**
- Sympa? Myriam? Je ne pense pas. Je la trouve désagréable.

3 Il est beau; il est mince; il a les cheveux bruns/il est brun, il fait un mètre quatre-vingts. Il est très sympa, gentil et drôle.

*1 chauves (bald); 2 sorry – désolé(e);
3 On pourrait aller au nouveau
restaurant français. 4 qui; 5 birthday;
6 si; 7 je ne sais pas (qui vient ce
soir); 8 C'est dommage, mais j'ai
quelquechose de prévu.*

Unit 10

Page 96 Following a recipe

2 • Alors, je t'explique comment on fait
le gratin dauphinois. Bon, d'abord,
je lave et j'épluche les pommes de
terre.
   ◆ Tu laves les pommes de terre avant
de les éplucher?
   • Oui, c'est ça. Je les coupe en petites
tranches très fines et je les mets
dans une casserole, avec un demi-
litre de lait, un peu de beurre et une
bonne pincée de noix de muscade.
   ◆ Et tu ajoutes aussi du sel et du
poivre?
   • Oui, bien sûr. Bon, je porte à
ébullition. Après, je baisse le feu
– je réduis à feu très doux, en
fait. Il faut remuer doucement les
pommes de terre – pendant cinq
minutes à peu près.
   ◆ Pourquoi?
   • Pour éviter que ça colle. Au bout
de cinq minutes, j'ajoute deux
cent cinquante grammes de crème
fraîche. Je laisse cuire tout ça à
feu doux, pendant environ cinq
minutes. Je continue de remuer
doucement de temps en temps. Au
bout de quelques minutes, je retire
la casserole du feu et j'ajoute deux
gousses d'ail écrasées.
   ◆ Tu penses que ça suffit?
   • Alors ça, c'est une question de goût.
Bon, ben après ça, c'est prêt. Je
verse le tout dans un plat – un plat
à gratin, naturellement. Je mets le
plat au four. Et voilà!

   ◆ À quelle température?
   • À cent quatre-vingts degrés.
   ◆ Et pour combien de temps?
   • Quarante minutes à peu près.
*1 éplucher; 2 mettre, poivrer; 3 baisser;
4 remuer; 5 cuire; 6 ajouter; 7 verser;
8 180°, 40.*

Page 97 Choosing wine to complement a dish

2 *entrées:* b, d, i; *plats principaux:* a, e, g;
desserts: c, f, h

3 • Qu'est-ce que tu as acheté comme
vins?
   ◆ J'ai choisi deux vins rouges, un
Côtes du Rhône et un Bourgogne.
Le vendeur m'a dit que le Côtes du
Rhône est robuste mais très fruité.
Il sera excellent avec le fromage.
Le Bourgogne ira très bien avec le
bœuf bourguignon, bien sûr. C'est
un vin moelleux.
   • Et les blancs?
   ◆ J'ai acheté des vins connus, que
tout le monde aimera, j'espère.
Le vendeur m'a recommandé un
Chablis, qui est un vin très sec mais
aussi fruité et légèrement acidulé.
J'ai choisi aussi un Sancerre, un vin
sec plutôt délicat. Je l'ai goûté, c'est
un vin très léger. Le Chablis ira bien
avec le poulet et le Sancerre sera
parfait avec le saumon.
   • Tu penses que ça suffit?
   ◆ Oui, oui, je pense; quatre sortes de
vin, ça suffit.
   • Bon, alors, on est prêt. Il faut mettre
les bouteilles au frigo?
   ◆ Non, non, pas le vin rouge!
Évidemment, il doit être servi
chambré. Le vin blanc, oui, il doit
être servi bien frais. J'ai déjà mis
quelques bouteilles au frigo.
*Côtes du Rhône: rouge, robuste, fruité
Bourgogne: rouge, moelleux
Chablis: blanc, sec, fruité, acidulé
Sancerre: blanc, sec, délicat, léger*

Page 98 Commenting on a meal

2 ● Tu as goûté le bœuf bourguignon?
  ◆ Oui, il est délicieux. J'aime bien les viandes au vin rouge.
  ● Tu bois quel vin?
  ◆ Celui-là – je te le conseille. Il est très léger.
  ● Il est robuste, ce vin, non?
  ◆ Oui, mais il est fruité et moelleux.
  ● Tu as aimé le saumon?
  ◆ Mmm ... parfait! Cuit à la perfection.
  ● Tu veux un morceau de gâteau?
  ◆ Non, merci, c'est un peu trop sucré à mon goût.
  ● Qu'est-ce que tu penses de la tarte au citron?
  ◆ Délicieuse, acidulée juste comme il faut!

  a 5; b 4; c 2; d 1; e 6; f 3.

3 ● Qu'est-ce que tu penses de la tarte au citron?
  ◆ Délicieuse, acidulée juste comme il faut! J'ai une passion pour la tarte au citron. Ça me rappelle les tartes que je mangeais chez **ma grand-mère quand j'étais petite. Tous les ans**, on allait passer **les grandes vacances** chez elle, à la campagne.
  Qui? Alice's grandmother.
  Quand? Every year/summer holiday when Alice was little.

Page 99 Expressing your appreciation

2 ● Merci à tous d'être venus. Je suis très très heureuse de vous voir tous ici, aujourd'hui. J'espère que vous vous êtes bien amusés. Le repas était parfait.
  ◆ Moi, j'ai passé une super soirée! Je voudrais souhaiter à Charlotte, en notre nom à tous, un joyeux anniversaire. Je te souhaite – nous te souhaitons tous – beaucoup de bonheur pour cette année ... et pour bien d'autres à venir!
  ● Bon anniversaire, Charlotte!
  Not mentioned: prosperity.

3 *She mentions seeing all her friends and the delicious food. Hugo: the gratin dauphinois. Adrien: contacting all their friends. Juliette: lending her flat.*

Page 100 Put it all together

1 *a 5; b 4; c 1; d 3; e 2.*

2 *Correct order: c, d, e, h, a, g, i, b, f.*

3 *a* future, *I will be; b* present, *I reply, I am replying; c* imperfect, *I used to go, I was going; d* present, *I do, I am doing; e* imperfect, *I was, I used to be; f* future, *I will eat; g* present, *I hope; h* present, *I see; i* future, *I will have; j* imperfect, *I used to work, I was working.*

Page 101 Now you're talking!

1 ● Tu aimes le gratin dauphinois?
  ◆ **C'est délicieux, cuit à la perfection.**
  ● Oui, je suis d'accord avec toi. Il est très bon.
  ◆ **Tu as goûté la salade niçoise?**
  ● Non, je n'aime pas tellement les olives: je vais prendre de la salade de tomates. Et le vin? Qu'est-ce que tu penses du Bourgogne?
  ◆ **Il est très bon, il est robuste et très fruité. Je l'aime bien.**

2 ● **Quel joli gâteau!**
  ◆ C'est moi qui l'ai fait. C'est une recette de ma mère. Il contient des amandes. J'espère que vous n'êtes pas allergique aux fruits secs.
  ● **Non, je ne suis pas allergique aux fruits secs.**
  ◆ Qu'est-ce que vous pensez de mon gâteau?
  ● **Il est délicieux. Je peux avoir la recette?**
  ◆ Oui, bien sûr, je vous la donnerai demain.

- Merci beaucoup, Claude. Je me suis bien amusé(e). Le gâteau était très bon. Au revoir.

Page 102 Quiz
1 une recette; 2 potatoes, plat à gratin; 3 éplucher; 4 the party will be great (sera – future tense); 5 bonheur; 6 j'avais; 7 onions; 8 on a bottle of red wine.

En plus 5
Pages 103–106

1 *a f, l'Allemagne et la Suisse; b f, elle a changé d'identité quatre fois; c f, ils vont souvent en Allemagne et en Suisse; d f, il n'y a pas de plages; e v; f v; g f, ses vins blancs.*

2 *a 3; b 1; c 2.*

3 • Bienvenue en France! Moi, je suis Ghislaine. Mon mari Gilles n'est malheureusement pas encore rentré du travail, mais je vous présente nos enfants Florian et Lucie.
   ♦ **Enchantée. Je m'appelle Liz, et je vous présente mon mari Tony, et mes enfants.**
   • Vous avez fait bon voyage?
   ♦ **Oui, on a fait bon voyage. Les trains sont très rapides.**
   • Vous êtes partis de chez vous à quelle heure ce matin?
   ♦ **On est partis à six heures et demie.**
   • Et il faisait quel temps en Angleterre ce matin?
   ♦ **Il faisait froid.**
   • Vous connaissez l'Alsace?
   ♦ **Je la connais un peu, j'ai passé une semaine à Strasbourg toute seule, il y a trois ans. L'année dernière, on est allés dans le Midi. Moi, j'adore la France et j'apprends le français depuis trois ans.**

4 • Alors, qu'est-ce que vous avez fait aujourd'hui?
   ♦ **On s'est promenés dans le centre de Colmar. On a acheté du vin et on est allés voir l'Église des Dominicains.**
   • Vous y avez vu le célèbre tableau 'La Vierge au buisson de roses'?
   ♦ **Oui, on l'a vu. Malheureusement on n'a pas de photos parce que Tony a perdu son appareil-photo. C'est dommage.**
   • C'est vrai? Vous avez fait une déclaration de perte?
   ♦ **Oui, on est allés au commissariat en face de l'office du tourisme.**
   • J'espère qu'on va le retrouver. Maintenant, vous voulez boire un apéritif?
   ♦ **Oui, volontiers.**

5 Chère Léa,
   On est arrivés en Alsace lundi. On habite chez une famille très sympa, dans une grande maison ancienne, en banlieue. Il y a du soleil.
   Mardi, on s'est levés tôt, il y a beaucoup à faire ici.
   Mercredi, on est allés voir un vignoble dans les Vosges. J'ai goûté à cinq vins différents, tous excellents. J'ai mangé de la choucroute dans un restaurant traditionnel.
   Jeudi, le groupe a fait le tour de Colmar. Quelle jolie ville! Malheureusement, je n'ai pas de photos parce que Tony a perdu son appareil-photo. Il a fait une déclaration au commissariat. On est rentrés tard à la maison. M et Mme Bertrand sont très gentils.
   Je me suis très bien amusée ici, j'aime beaucoup l'Alsace et je vais revenir en France l'année prochaine!
   Amitiés, Liz

pronunciation and spelling

1 Vowel sounds

a	bad		u	position lips to say **oo**ze, then try saying **ea**se without moving the lips
e	brother			
(before two consonants)	egg		ai	day
é	day		eu	girl
ê, è	egg		oi	wag
i	east		au, eau	over
o	hot or over		ou	ooze

- **y** is a vowel in French; it is pronounced as in **ea**st.

- **Accents** over an **e** change its sound but otherwise a circumflex (^) or a grave accent (`) make no difference to pronunciation. Accents can differentiate between two words which look and sound the same: **ou** or, **où** where, **a** has, **à** to, at.

- **Nasal vowels** Vowels followed by **m** or **n** are usually nasal (unless there's another vowel following the **m** or **n**, as in **ami**, **dîner**). The tongue doesn't touch the roof of the mouth (**n**), and the lips don't close (**m**), but instead air is expelled through the mouth and nose: **un, faim, vin**.

2 Consonant sounds

c	cat before a, o, u		j	leisure
	sat before e, i, y		ll	usually well (**elle**)
ç	sat			sometimes kiosk (**fille**)
ch	shoe			(y pronounced)
g	golf before a, o, u		qu	card
	leisure before e, i		r	like Scottish loch; 'gargled' in back of throat
gn	canyon			
h	always silent		th	tea

- Usually, the final consonant of a French word is not sounded: **chat** is pronounced 'cha', **chaud** is pronounced 'chau'.

- However, if the following word starts with a vowel or silent h, you do usually sound the last consonant:
  Vous êtes français? (pronounced vou**z**êtes français?)
  Il est anglais. (pronounced Il es**t**anglais)

numbers and dates

0 zéro	21 vingt et un	100 cent
1 un/une	22 vingt-deux	101 cent un
2 deux	23 vingt-trois	200 deux cents**
3 trois	24 vingt-quatre	201 deux cent un
4 quatre	25 vingt-cinq	1000 mille
5 cinq	26 vingt-six	2000 deux mille
6 six	27 vingt-sept	2001 deux mille un
7 sept	28 vingt-huit	1.000.000 un million
8 huit	29 vingt-neuf	2.000.000 deux millions
9 neuf	30 trente*	
10 dix	40 quarante	
11 onze	50 cinquante	
12 douze	60 soixante	
13 treize	70 soixante-dix	
14 quatorze	71 soixante et onze	1st premier
15 quinze	72 soixante-douze	2nd deuxième
16 seize	80 quatre-vingts	3rd troisième
17 dix-sept	81 quatre-vingt-un	
18 dix-huit	82 quatre-vingt-deux	
19 dix-neuf	90 quatre-vingt-dix	
20 vingt	91 quatre-vingt-onze	
	92 quatre-vingt-douze	

- * 31–99 follow the same pattern as 21–29: **trente et un, trente-deux** etc.
- ** Only the round hundreds have an **-s**.
- **Un** becomes **une** when it refers to a feminine noun: **mille et une nuits, vingt et une étudiantes**.

lundi Monday	vendredi Friday
mardi Tuesday	samedi Saturday
mercredi Wednesday	dimanche Sunday
jeudi Thursday	

janvier January	mai May	septembre September
février February	juin June	octobre October
mars March	juillet July	novembre November
avril April	août August	décembre December

- Days and months are all masculine. Dates are written **le 3 mai** and said **le trois mai**, except for the first of the month: **le premier juin**.

grammar

This section uses the key grammatical terms defined on page 6.

G1 **Nouns** are all either masculine (m) or feminine (f). Sometimes the gender can be deduced from the ending.
- Nouns ending -**age**, -**al**, -**é**, -**eau**, -**eu**, -**ier**, -**isme**, -**ment** are generally <u>masculine</u> (but l'**eau** and la **plage** are feminine).
- Nouns ending -**ée**, -**euse**, **ière**, -**tion**, or any double consonant followed by a silent **e** (e.g. -**tte**) are generally <u>feminine</u>.

Most nouns add an -**s** to form the plural:

le restaurant ▸ les restaurants	la maison ▸ les maisons
l'homme ▸ les hommes	l'ami ▸ les amis

- Nouns ending in -al and -ail become -**aux** in the plural:

l'animal ▸ les animaux	le travail ▸ les travaux

- Nouns ending in -eu and -eau add -**x** in the plural:

le feu ▸ les feux	le gâteau ▸ les gâteaux

- Nouns ending in -s, -x or -z don't change in the plural:

le fils ▸ les fils	le prix ▸ les prix	le nez ▸ les nez

G2 **Articles** have masculine and feminine, singular and plural forms.

	a/an	*the*	*some/any*
m sing	**un** jour	**le** jour	**du** vin
f sing	**une** maison	**la** maison	**de la** bière
before vowel or silent h	**une** église **un** hôtel	**l'**église **l'**hôtel	**de l'**eau
plural		**les** maisons **les** enfants	**des** maisons **des** enfants

Use **de** instead of **un/une/du/de la/de l'/des** after a negative:
Il y a <u>un</u> balcon et <u>des</u> terrasses mais il n'y a <u>pas de</u> garage.
Use **de** instead of **des** when followed by adjective + noun:
des plages but **de grandes plages**.

G3 The **prepositions** à and de are translated in several different ways:
- à *at* à l'aéroport, à deux heures *in* j'habite à York
   to je vais à l'aéroport *on/by* à pied, à vélo

à can't be followed by **le** or **les**; they combine to form **au** and **aux** respectively: **je vais au travail; il habite aux États-Unis.**

- de *from* il vient de Martinique *from* de dix heures à midi
   of une bouteille de vin *per* cinq euros de l'heure
   of (possession) le mari de ma sœur

de can't be followed by **le** or **les**; they combine to form **du** and **des**.

G4 Adjectives change to agree with what they describe.

- Most adjectives follow a pattern: add -**e** to the masculine singular to form the feminine and add -**s** to form the plural.

  le sac noir ▸ les sacs noirs　　**la veste noire ▸ les vestes noires**

- Adjectives already ending in -**e** or -**s** don't add another one:

  le sac rouge ▸ la veste rouge　　**le vin français ▸ les vins français**

- Other masculine/feminine patterns:

  -**er ▸ -ère**　　**premier/première**
  -**f ▸ -ve**　　**neuf/neuve**
  -**x ▸ -se**　　**heureux/heureuse**

Some double the last consonant before adding -**e**: **italien/italienne**.

- Another singular/plural pattern:

  -**al ▸ -aux**　　**local/locale ▸ locaux/locales**

Some irregular adjectives:

m sing	f sing	m pl	f pl
beau*	belle	beaux	belles
blanc	blanche	blancs	blanches
long	longue	longs	longues
nouveau*	nouvelle	nouveaux	nouvelles
vieux*	vieille	vieux	vieilles

*beau, nouveau and vieux have a special masculine form before a vowel or silent h, **bel, nouvel, vieil: un nouvel hôtel, un vieil homme.**

G5 Position of adjectives When adjectives and nouns are next to each other

- most adjectives go <u>after</u> the noun: **un gîte <u>confortable</u>, la chemise <u>bleue</u>**
- several common adjectives like **grand**, **petit**, **joli**, **beau**, **bon** and **nouveau**, go <u>before</u> the noun: **un <u>grand</u> gîte, une <u>jolie</u> ville**
- **premier, deuxième, troisième**, etc. also go before the noun: **au <u>deuxième</u> étage**

G6 Possessive adjectives agree with the gender of what's owned, not the owner. *My house* is always **ma maison.**

	m sing*	f sing	plural
my	mon	ma	mes
your **tu**	ton	ta	tes
his/her	son	sa	ses
our	notre	notre	nos
your **vous**	votre	votre	vos
their	leur	leur	leurs

* and f sing before vowel or silent h

G7 Ce *this, that*:
- goes before the noun and agrees with it:
  ce restaurant, **cette maison**, **ces brochures**
- has a special masculine singular form used before a vowel or silent h:
  cet homme, **cet été**
- add -**ci** *this* or -**là** *that* for emphasis:
  ce vin-ci *this wine*; **cette chemise-là** *that shirt*

G8 Celui-ci and celui-là mean *this one, that one*.
- **Celle-ci** and **celle-là** are the feminine versions.
  Je vais prendre celui-ci. *I'll take this one.* (masculine item)
  Je préfère celle-là. *I prefer that one.* (feminine item)
- **ceux** is the masculine plural form and **celles** the feminine plural:
  Je préfère ceux-ci. *I prefer these (ones).*

G9 Adverbs often end in -**ment** (equivalent to -**ly** in English), which is added to a feminine adjective: <u>heureusement</u> *luckily*, <u>rapidement</u> *quickly*, <u>seulement</u> *only*. The ending of an adverb doesn't change.
- A few adverbs are formed from a masculine adjective instead:
  <u>vraiment</u> *really*, <u>absolument</u> *absolutely*.
- Other common adverbs include **très** *very*, **trop** *too*, **plutôt** *rather*, **assez** *quite*, **un peu** *a bit*, **si** *so*, **vite** *quickly*.

G10 Comparison Add **plus** *more* and **moins** *less* to adjectives and adverbs to compare two or more things: **plus agréable** *nicer*, **plus moulant** *more clingy*, **moins cher** *less expensive*, **moins vite** *less quickly*.
- *Than* is **que**: **La veste est plus chère que le pantalon.** *The jacket is more expensive than the trousers.*
- **Le/la/les** + **plus/moins** means *the most* or *the least*: **le costume le plus élégant** *the most stylish suit*, **la veste la moins chère** *the least expensive jacket*.

G11 Verbs There are three main groups of verbs, ending in -**er**, -**ir**, -**re** in the infinitive (*to do*). The -**er**, -**ir**, -**re** ending changes in a predictable, regular way according to:
- subject: <u>who/what</u> is carrying out the verb,
- tense: <u>when</u> it takes place.

G12 Subject pronouns **je**, **tu**, **il**, **elle**, **on**, **nous**, **vous**, **ils** and **elles** show who or what is carrying out the verb.
- There are two words for *you*, each of which uses a different verb ending:
  tu: when talking to one person who is a friend or relative, or a child; young people usually use **tu** with each other from the start.
  vous: when talking to one person you don't know very well, or who is older than you. Use it also when talking to more than one person.

- **Il** and **elle** both mean *it*, as well as *he* or *she*; use **il** when a masculine noun is meant and **elle** a feminine noun.
- **On** is used a lot in spoken French to mean *we*, *they*, or *you* (people in general). It takes the same verb endings as **il** and **elle**.

3 Present tense
- The equivalent of *do, am/is/are doing*.
- With **depuis**, it means *have been doing*: **Je travaille ici depuis six mois/ depuis septembre.** *I've been working here for six months/since September.*
- Regular -**er**, -**re** and -**ir** verbs follow the patterns shown below.

	aim**er**	vend**re**	fin**ir**
je, j'	aim**e**	vend**s**	fin**is**
tu	aim**es**	vend**s**	fin**is**
il, elle, on	aim**e**	vend	fin**it**
nous	aim**ons**	vend**ons**	fin**issons**
vous	aim**ez**	vend**ez**	fin**issez**
ils, elles	aim**ent**	vend**ent**	fin**issent**

- Some -ir verbs such as **partir**, **sortir** and **dormir** follow a different pattern from above, with shorter singular forms and omitting the -**iss** in the plural form: **je sors**, **nous sortons**.
- Verbs ending in -**ger**/-**cer** preserve the soft sound in the **nous** form by adding an -**e** before -**ons** (-**ger** verbs) or changing the -**c** to a -**ç**: **nous mangeons, nous nageons, nous commençons**.

4 Irregular verbs
Not all verbs follow the regular patterns. The following common verbs are irregular in the present tense.

	je, j'	tu	il, elle, on	nous	vous	ils, elles
aller *to go*	vais	vas	va	allons	allez	vont
avoir *to have*	ai	as	a	avons	avez	ont
boire *to drink*	bois	bois	boit	buvons	buvez	boivent
connaître *to know*	connais	connais	connaît	connaissons	connaissez	connaissent
devoir *to have to*	dois	dois	doit	devons	devez	doivent
dire *to say*	dis	dis	dit	disons	dites	disent
écrire *to write*	écris	écris	écrit	écrivons	écrivez	écrivent
être *to be*	suis	es	est	sommes	êtes	sont
faire *to do, to make*	fais	fais	fait	faisons	faites	font
pouvoir *to be able to*	peux	peux	peut	pouvons	pouvez	peuvent

prendre *to take*	prends	prends	prend	prenons	prenez	prenner
savoir *to know*	sais	sais	sait	savons	savez	savent
venir *to come*	viens	viens	vient	venons	venez	viennen
voir *to see*	vois	vois	voit	voyons	voyez	voient
vouloir *to want to*	veux	veux	veut	voulons	voulez	veulent

- **apprendre** *to learn* and **comprendre** *to understand* behave like **prendre**.
- **revenir** *to come back* and **devenir** *to become* behave like **venir**.

G15 Il faut is an impersonal verb, in other words, there is only an **il** form, regardless of who is being referred to. It is always followed by an infinitive: **il faut partir** *I/you/we must leave.*

G16 The verbs **avoir**, **faire** and **aller** appear in many useful expressions.
- **avoir besoin de** *to need*, **avoir peur** *to be afraid*, **avoir envie de** *to feel like*, **avoir raison/tort** *to be right/wrong*, **avoir faim/soif** *to be hungry/thirsty*, **avoir chaud/froid** *to be hot/cold*, **avoir de la chance** *to be lucky*
- to express age: **elle a 30 ans** *she's 30 years old*
- **il y a** *there is, there are*
- weather: **il y a du soleil/du vent** *it's sunny/windy*
- **Qu'est-ce que tu as?** *What's the matter?*
- **avoir mal**: **j'ai mal à la tête** *I've got a headache.*

- sports and leisure activities: **faire une randonnée** *to go for a walk*, **faire du ski/de la voile/de l'exercice** *to go skiing/sailing/to do some exercise*
- **faire mal** means *to hurt*: **ça fait mal** *that hurts*
- **faire 1,80 m** *to be 1.8 m tall*, **faire 60 kg** *to weigh 60 kg*, **faire du 40** *to be size 40*
- weather: **il fait chaud/mauvais** *it's warm/bad weather*

- health: **comment allez-vous?** *how are you?* **Je ne vais pas bien** *I'm not well.*
- to say something suits someone: **Il me va?** *Does it suit me?*

G17 Aller + infinitive You can talk about the near future using the present tense of **aller** followed by an infinitive – the equivalent of *going to do ...*
Qu'est-ce que tu vas faire? *What are you going to do?*
Je vais inviter mes amis. *I'm going to invite my friends.*

G18 Future tense
- The equivalent of *will do* or *shall do*.
- There's always an **-r** immediately before the ending.
- For many verbs, add the endings in bold below on to the infinitive. For **-re** verbs, drop the final **-e**.

	aimer	vendre	partir
je, j'	aimerai	vendrai	partirai
tu	aimeras	vendras	partiras
il, elle, on	aimera	vendra	partira
nous	aimerons	vendrons	partirons
vous	aimerez	vendrez	partirez
ils, elles	aimeront	vendront	partiront

- Irregular verbs have the same endings as above, but they follow a different first part, not formed from the infinitive:

  aller: j'irai, tu iras, ...
  avoir: j'aurai, tu auras, ...
  devoir: je devrai, tu devras, ...
  être: je serai, tu seras, ...
  faire: je ferai, tu feras, ...

  pouvoir: je pourrai, tu pourras, ...
  venir: je viendrai, tu viendras, ...
  voir: je verrai, tu verras, ...
  vouloir: je voudrai, tu voudras, ...

19 Conditional

- The equivalent of *would do*.
- Used in polite requests: **je voudrais** *I'd like*, **on pourrait ...** *we could ...*
- The first part is the same as for the future tense[18], and the endings are the same as for the imperfect tense[20].

aimer:	future	**j'aimerai**	*I will like*
	imperfect	**j'aimais**	*I used to like*
	conditional	**j'aimerais**	*I would like*

20 Imperfect tense

- The equivalent of *was/were doing* and *used to do*.
- Formed from the **nous** part of the present tense; take off the final **-ons** and replace it with the endings shown in bold:

	aimer (aimons)	vendre (vendons)	finir (finissons)
je, j'	aimais	vendais	finissais
tu	aimais	vendais	finissais
il, elle, on	aimait	vendait	finissait
nous	aimions	vendions	finissions
vous	aimiez	vendiez	finissiez
ils, elles	aimaient	vendaient	finissaient

- There is only one irregular verb in this tense: **être: j'étais, tu étais,** ...
- Other verbs that are irregular in the present tense still use their **nous** form for the imperfect:

  faire: present **nous faisons** ▸ imperfect **il faisait chaud** *it was hot*
  avoir: present **nous avons** ▸ imperfect **j'avais** *I had*, **il y avait** *there was/were*

G21 **Perfect tense**

- The equivalent of *did* or *have done*.
- Most verbs form the perfect tense with the present tense of **avoir** + the past participle[22] of the main verb.
- A few verbs, mainly relating to movement[24], use the present tense of **être** instead of **avoir**. Reflexive verbs[25] also use **être**.

G22 **Past participles** (pp) are formed from an infinitive by changing:

-**er** to -**é**: **travailler** ▸ **travaillé**
-**ir** to -**i**: **finir** ▸ **fini**
-**re** to -**u**: **vendre** ▸ **vendu**

Many common verbs have an irregular past participle, including these:

avoir *to have*	pp **eu**	**lire** *to read*	pp **lu**
boire *to drink*	pp **bu**	**mettre** *to put*	pp **mis**
dire *to say*	pp **dit**	**offrir** *to offer*	pp **offert**
écrire *to write*	pp **écrit**	**ouvrir** *to open*	pp **ouvert**
être *to be*	pp **été**	**prendre** *to take*	pp **pris**
faire *to do/make*	pp **fait**	**voir** *to see*	pp **vu**

- **apprendre** *to learn* and **comprendre** *to understand* behave like **prendre**: pp **appris/compris**.

G23 **Perfect tense with avoir**

j'	**ai**	
tu	**as**	
il, elle, on	**a**	**travaillé**
nous	**avons**	
vous	**avez**	
ils, elles	**ont**	

G24 **Perfect tense with être** The ending of the pp agrees with the subject.

		m	f
je	**suis**	**allé**	**allée**
tu	**es**	**allé**	**allée**
il	**est**	**allé**	–
elle	**est**	–	**allée**
on	**est**	**allé, allés**	**allée, allées**
nous	**sommes**	**allés**	**allées**
vous	**êtes**	**allé, allés**	**allée, allées**
ils	**sont**	**allés**	–
elles	**sont**	–	**allées**

The following are the most common **être** verbs. The past participle is listed only where it is irregular.

aller *to go*	**partir** *to leave/depart*
arriver *to arrive*	**rentrer** *to go/return home*
descendre *to go down, get off*	**rester** *to stay/remain*
entrer *to enter*	**retourner** *to return*
monter *to go up, climb*	**sortir** *to go out*
mourir *to die* (pp **mort**)	**tomber** *to fall*
naître *to be born* (pp **né**)	**venir** *to come* (pp **venu**)

- **revenir** *to return*, **devenir** *to become* behave like **venir** (pp **revenu/devenu**).
- All reflexive verbs[25] use **être** to form the perfect tense.

25   **Reflexive verbs** The infinitive of these verbs includes **se** or **s'**: **s'appeler** *to be called*, **se lever** *to get up*, **se reposer** *to rest*. They follow the usual pattern of endings, with **me**, **te**, **se** , **nous** or **vous** before the verb, according to who/what is involved.

	present	perfect
je	**me repose**	**me suis reposé(e)**
tu	**te repose**	**t'es reposé(e)**
il, elle	**se repose**	**s'est reposé(e)**
on	**se repose**	**s'est reposé(e)s**
nous	**nous reposons**	**nous sommes reposé(e)s**
vous	**vous reposez**	**vous êtes reposé(e)(s)(es)**
ils, elles	**se reposent**	**se sont reposé(e)s**

26   **Imperatives** are used to give directions or instructions. They are usually the same as the **tu** or **vous** present tense, with the subject pronoun omitted. When the **tu** form ends -**es** or -**as**, the imperative drops the -**s** (except before **y** or **en**: **vas-y** *go on/go there*). Reflexive verbs add -**toi** or -**vous** after the verb.

	tu	vous
écouter	**écoute**	**écoutez**
répondre	**réponds**	**répondez**
prendre	**prends**	**prenez**
aller	**va**	**allez**
se reposer	**repose-toi**	**reposez-vous**

- You'll see the **infinitive** used instead of the imperative in written instructions: **prendre deux comprimés** *take two tablets*, and in recipes: **éplucher les pommes de terre** *peel the potatoes*.
- **Il faut** and **devoir** + infinitive are other ways of giving instructions: **Il faut/Vous devez continuer tout droit**.

G27 **Negatives** To make a negative statement, **ne ... pas** goes around the verb. In the perfect tense, it goes around the part of **avoir** or **être**. With reflexive verbs, **me**, **te**, **se**, etc. go inside **ne ... pas**.

Elle n'a pas d'enfants.   **Je n'ai pas vu ce film.**
Je ne me lève pas tôt le samedi.   **Je ne me suis pas levé tôt hier.**

- **Ne** is used with negative words like **jamais** *never*, **rien** *nothing*, **personne** *nobody*, **ni ... ni** *neither ... nor*:
  Je ne mange jamais de viande. *I never eat meat.*
  Elle n'a plus d'argent. *She hasn't got any more money.*
  Il n'est ni grand ni petit. *He's neither tall nor short.*
- With a perfect tense verb, **ne plus**, **ne rien** and **ne jamais** just go round the part of **avoir** or **être**:
  Je n'ai rien vu. *I saw nothing/I didn't see anything.*
  But **ne personne** and **ne que** go round the past participle too:
  Je n'ai mangé qu'un sandwich. *I've only eaten a sandwich.*

G28 **Verbs followed by an infinitive**
Some key verbs can be followed immediately by an infinitive:
devoir: Vous devez aller tout droit.   **pouvoir: On peut jouer au tennis.**
savoir: Je sais faire une omelette.   **vouloir: Tu veux aller au bar?**
aimer: J'aime faire du ski.   **espérer: J'espère revenir bientôt.**

- Some verbs need **à** before the following infinitive:
  apprendre à *to learn*: **J'apprends à danser.**
  commencer à *to begin*: **Je commence à comprendre.**
- Some verbs need **de** before the infinitive that follows:
  avoir envie de: J'ai envie d'aller au restaurant.
  conseiller de: Je vous conseille de réserver.

G29 **Questions** can be formed with a question word (see page 25):
Qui? *Who/Whom?* **Où?** *Where?* **Quand?** *When?* **Comment?** *How?*
Pourquoi? *Why?* **Que ...?** *What ...?* **Qu'est-ce que ...?** *What?*
Quel(le) ...? *Which ...?* **Combien de ...?** *How much ...? How many ...?*

- They can also be formed by making your voice go up at the end of a statement so that it sounds like a question.
- Or by adding **est-ce que** ... before a statement or after a question word:
  Est-ce que vous êtes français? Où est-ce que vous habitez?

G30 **Quel** is a question word meaning *which...?* or *what ...?* used with a noun.

	singular	plural
m	**quel gîte?**	**quels gîtes?**
f	**quelle maison?**	**quelles maisons?**

It also means *what a ...!* in an exclamation: **quelle jolie ville!** *what a lovely town!*

31 **Lequel?** *which one?* can replace a phrase comprised of **quel** + a noun. When the item isn't specified, its gender is still reflected in the form used:
lequel?/laquelle?/lesquels?/lesquelles?
Vous avez vu le nouveau film italien? – Lequel?
Regarde les bottes noires et les bottes marron: lesquelles tu préfères?

32 **Object pronouns** When the object of a verb (the person or thing affected) is a pronoun and not a named person/item, it can be direct (e.g. *me, him, us*) or indirect (e.g. *to me, to him, to us*). In French, only the words for 'him/her/it' have different forms for direct and indirect:

direct		indirect	
me	*me*	**me**	*to me*
te	*you*	**te**	*to you*
le, l'	*him/it*	**lui**	*to him*
la, l'	*her/it*	**lui**	*to her*
nous	*us*	**nous**	*to us*
vous	*you*	**vous**	*to you*
les	*them*	**leur**	*to them*

- Both sets normally go in front of the relevant verb:
Je voudrais l'essayer. *I'd like to try it on.* **Je ne les connais pas.** *I don't know them.* **Il m'a dit ...** *He told me (said to me) ...* **Je peux vous aider?** *Can I help you?*

33 **Emphatic pronouns moi, toi, lui, elle, nous, vous, eux, elles** are used
- for emphasis: **Moi, j'aime la veste bleue, mais lui, il préfère la grise.**
- after a preposition: **avec moi, pour nous, chez eux.**

34 **Y** is a pronoun meaning *there*. It comes before the verb.
Tu connais Nice? Oui, j'y suis allé en juin. *Do you know Nice? Yes, I went there in June.*

35 **En** is a pronoun meaning *of it/them* or *some/any*. It comes before the verb.
Il y a combien de chambres? Il y en a trois. *How many bedrooms? There are three (of them).*
Vous avez des analgésiques? Oui, j'en ai. *Have you any painkillers? Yes, I've got some.*

36 **Qui** and **que** are pronouns meaning *who, whom, which, that.* Both can be used for people and for things. **Qui** is used when it's the subject of the following verb, and **que** when it's the object.
Il y a un train qui part à midi. *There's a train which leaves at midday.*
J'ai une copine qui habite à Paris. *I have a friend who lives in Paris.*
Voici l'acteur que je préfère. *Here's the actor who/that I prefer.*

French–English glossary

This glossary contains the words found in this book, with their meanings in the contexts used here. Most verbs are given only in the infinitive, but parts of some French irregular verbs are also included. Regular adjectives are listed in the masculine singular version; for irregular adjectives, the feminine endings are also listed. Abbreviations: (m) masculine, (f) feminine, (sing) singular, (pl) plural, (n) noun, (adj) adjective, (adv) adverb.

A

absolument really
accepté accepted
accepter to accept
accident (m) accident
accord: d'accord OK, agreed
acheter to buy
acidulé acidic
acteur (m) actor
activité (f) activity
adorer to adore
adresse (f) address
adulte (m/f) adult
aéroport (m) airport
affreux/euse terrible
actrice (f) actress
Afrique (f) Africa
âge (m) age
âgé elderly
agence immobilière (f) estate agent's
agent (m/f) de police police officer
agent immobilier (m) estate agent
agréable nice, pleasant
aider to help
aigle (m) eagle
ail (m) garlic
aimable nice
aimer to like
ajouter to add
ajustable adjustable
alcool (m) alcohol
alentours (m pl) outskirts
Algérie (f) Algeria
Allemagne (f) Germany
allemand German
Allemand(e) (m/f) German
aller to go, suit
allergie (f) allergy

allergique allergic
allô hello (on phone)
alors well, then
Alpes (f pl) Alps
alsacien(ne) from Alsace, Alsatian
amande (f) almond
aménagements (m pl) facilities
américain American
Américain(e) (m/f) American
Amérique du Sud (f) South America
ami(e) (m/f) friend
amitiés (f pl) all the best
amoureux/euse (m) lover
s'amuser to enjoy oneself
an (m) year
analgésique (m) painkiller
ancien(ne) old, former
anglais English
Anglais(e) (m/f) Englishman/woman
Angleterre (f) England
angoisse (f) anxiety, distress
animal (m) animal
animateur/trice (m/f) organiser of activities
année (f) year
anniversaire (m) birthday
anniversaire (m) de mariage wedding anniversary
annonce (f) advert
appareil (m) phone
appareil-photo (m) camera
appartement (m) flat
appeler to call, phone
s'appeler to be called
application (f) application
apporter to bring

apprendre to learn
après after
après-midi (m) afternoon
arboré planted with trees
architecte (m/f) architect
architecture (f) architecture
argent (m) money
arrêt (m) bus stop
arrêter, s'arrêter to stop
arrhes (f pl) deposit
arriver to arrive, happen
artichaut (m) artichoke
arts martiaux (m pl) martial arts
ascenseur (m) lift
aspirateur (m) vacuum cleaner
asseyez-vous (from s'asseoir) sit down
assez quite, enough
athlète (m/f) athlete
attache (f) fastening
attaché(e) de presse (m/f) press officer
atteindre to reach
attendre to wait (for)
aubaine (f) bargain
auberge de jeunesse (f) youth hostel
aujourd'hui today
aurai, aura (from avoir) will have
aussi too, also
autre other
Autriche (f) Austria
avance advance
    à l'avance, d'avance in advance
avant before
    à l'avant in front
avec with

averse (f) shower *(of rain)*
avis (m) opinion
   à mon avis in my
   opinion
avoir (pp eu) to have

B

se baigner to swim, bathe
baignoire (f) bath
baisser to lower
balcon (m) balcony
banc (m) bench
banlieue (f) outskirts
banque (f) bank
bar (m) bar
basilic (m) basil
baskets (f pl) trainers
bateau (m) boat
battre to beat, whisk
beau/belle beautiful
beaucoup (de) a lot (of)
beauté (f) beauty
belge Belgian
belle beautiful
belle-fille (f) daughter-
in-law
besoin need
   avoir besoin de to need
beurre (m) butter
bien sûr certainly, of
course
bien well, a lot
bien-être (m) well-being
bienfaisant beneficial
bienfait (m) benefit
bientôt soon
   à bientôt see you soon,
   bye for now
bienvenue welcome
billet (m) ticket, banknote
bip sonore (m) beep
bisou (m) kiss
blanc/blanche white
bleu (m) bruise
bleu (adj) blue
blond blond
blouson (m) short jacket
bœuf (m) beef
boire (pp bu) to drink
bon(ne) good
   bon courage all the best
bonheur (m) happiness

bord (m): au bord d'une
rivière on the riverbank
   bord de la mer seaside
botte (f) boot
bouche (f) mouth
boue (f) mud
bouilloire (f) kettle
bouillon: au premier
bouillon when it begins
to boil
boulangerie (f) baker's
boules (f pl) bowls
boussole (f) compass
bout (m) end
bouteille (f)
bouton (m) button
bras (m) arm
brasserie (f) restaurant
Brésil (m) Brazil
Bretagne (f) Brittany
britannique British
bronzer to sunbathe, tan
brouillard (m) fog
brun brown, dark-haired
buffle (m) buffalo
buisson (m) bush
bureau (m) office
bureau de poste (m) post
office

C

ça, cela that
cachemire (m) cashmere
cadeau (m) present
café (m) cafe, coffee
   café (m) au lait white
   coffee
calendrier (m) calendar
calme (m) peace and quiet
calme (adj) peaceful
camarade (m/f) de classe
classmate
campagne (f) countryside
camping (m) campsite
canapé-lit (m) sofa bed
capitale (f) capital
carrefour (m) crossroads
carte (f) map
carte bancaire (f) bank card
carte d'abonné/
d'abonnement season
ticket

carte (f) de crédit credit
card
carte (f) d'identité identity
card
cas: en tout cas in any case
casque (m) helmet
cassé broken
casserole (f) saucepan
cause: à cause de because
of
ce/cette this, that
ceinture (f) belt
célèbre famous
celle-ci, celle-là this one,
that one (f)
celui-ci, celui-là this one,
that one (m)
centre-ville (m) town
centre
cerise (f) cherry
cerisier (m) cherry tree
cette this, that
chacun each *(person)*
chambre (f) bedroom
chambre d'hôte (f) B&B
chambré at room
temperature
chance (f) luck
   avoir de la chance to be
   lucky
changement (m) change
changer to change
chanteur/euse (m/f) singer
chapeau (m) hat
chaque each
charcuterie (f) cold meats,
delicatessen
charme (m) charm
château (m) castle
chaud warm
chauffage central (m)
(central) heating
chauffé heated
chauffer to heat
chaussures de marche
(f pl) walking shoes
chauve bald
chef (m) boss
chemin de fer (m) railway
cheminée (f) chimney,
fireplace
chemise (f) shirt

cher/chère dear, expensive
chercher to look for
cheveux (m pl) hair
cheville (f) ankle
chez at the house of
chien (m) dog
chinois Chinese
chiropraxie chiropractic
chocolat (m) chocolate
choisir to choose
choix (m) choice
choucroute (m) sauerkraut
cidre (m) cider
cinéma (m) cinema
circonstances (f pl) circumstances
citron (m) lemon
clair light (colour)
classe (f) class
classe (adj) great
clé (f) key
climat (m) climate
clos enclosed
coiffeur/euse (m/f) hairdresser
coin (m) corner
collège (m) school
collègue (m/f) colleague
coller to stick
collier (m) collar
colline (f) hill
colloque (m) academic conference
colonie de vacances (f) holiday camp
combien (de) how much/many
commander to order
comme as
    comme il faut right, correctly
commencer to begin
comment how, what like
commercer to do business
commissariat (m) (de police) police station
communiquer to communicate
compagne (f) partner
compagnon (m) partner
compartiment (m) compartment

compatible compatible
complet/complète full
complètement completely
complexe sportif (m) sports centre
comprendre (pp compris) to understand
comprimé (m) tablet
comptable (m/f) accountant
compter to plan
confiance (f) confidence, trust
confort (m) comfort
confortable comfortable
congélateur (m) freezer
connaître to know
connu known
conquérir to overcome
conseiller to advise
contacter to contact
contenir to contain
contenu (m) contents
continent (m) continent
continuer to continue
contusion (f) bruise
convenir to suit
    si cela vous convient if that's OK with you
conversation (f) conversation
coordonner to match
copin(e) (m/f) friend
Corse (f) Corsica
costume (m) suit
côte (f) coast
côté: à côté de next to
coton (m) cotton
cou (m) neck
se coucher to go to bed
couleur (f) colour
coup: d'un seul coup all at once
couper to cut
couple (m) couple, pair
courage: bon courage all the best
cours (m) course, class
court short
cousin(e) (m/f) cousin
coûter to cost
couvert covered

créateur/trice (m/f) designer
crème solaire (f) sun cream
crois (from croire) (I) think
cuire (pp cuit) to cook
cuisine (f) cookery, kitchen
cuisinier/ière (m/f) cook
cuit cooked
curatif/ive healing (adj)
cure (f) spa treatment

D

d'abord first of all
d'accord OK, agreed
dangereux/euse dangerous
dans in
danser to dance
date (f) date
dater to date
débardeur (m) sleeveless top
décider to decide
déclaration (f) de perte lost property report
    faire une déclaration report an incident
découvrir to discover
décrire to describe
déçu disappointed
dégoûtant disgusting
degré (m) degree
dégustation (f) tasting
déjà already
déjeuner to have lunch
délégué (m) delegate
délicat delicate
délicieux/euse delicious
demain tomorrow
demi(e) half
dent (f) tooth
département (m) department
dépasser to exceed
dépendance (f) outhouse
dépliant (m) leaflet
dépression (f) depression
depuis since, for
dernier last
se dérouler to take place
désagréable unpleasant
descendre to go down, get off (a vehicle)

désert (m) desert
désolé sorry
dessert (m) dessert
détail (m) detail
deuxième second
devenir (pp devenu) to become
devoir to have to
différent different
dimensions (f pl) size
dîner (m) dinner
dîner to have dinner
diplômé qualified
dire (pp dit) to say
directeur/trice (m/f) director
discours (m) speech
discuter to discuss
disponible available
distributeur (m) de billets cashpoint
dites (from dire) tell me
diversité (f) diversity
divorcé divorced
docteur (m) doctor
doigt (m) finger
domicile: à domicile in your own home
domination (f) domination
dommage: c'est dommage it's a pity
donc therefore
donner to give
dos (m) back
dose (f) dose
doublure (f) lining
douche (f) shower
douleur (f) pain
douloureux/euse painful
doux/douce gentle
drap (m) sheet
dressing (m) dressing room, walk-in cupboard
droit: tout droit straight ahead
droite: à droite on/to the right
drôle amusing, funny
durablement enduringly
durée (f) duration
durer to last

E

eau (f) water
eau minérale (f) mineral water
ébullition (f) boiling point
échange (m) swap
échanger to change, exchange
éclaircie (f) sunny interval
école (f) school
écologie (f) ecology
Écosse (f) Scotland
écouter to listen (to)
écraser to crush
écrire (pp écrit) to write
écurie (f) stable
efficace effective
église (f) church
électrique electric
électro-ménager (m sing) electrical goods
élégant elegant, stylish
emblème (m) symbol
emplacement (m) site, spot
employé(e) (m/f) employee, clerk
en some, of them
enceinte pregnant
enchanté pleased to meet you
encore yet
endroit (m) place
énergétique energy (adj)
enfant (m/f) child
enfin well, at last
ensemble together
ensuite then
entendre to hear
entier/ière whole
entièrement entirely
entraîneur (m) trainer, coach
entre between
entrée (f) starter
entrer to enter, go in
entretien (f) interview
envahir to invade
envie: avoir envie de to feel like
environ about, approximately

environnement (m) environment
environs (m pl) outskirts
envoyer to send
épaule (f) shoulder
épinards (m pl) spinach
éplucher to peel
équipé equipped
équitation (f) horse riding
escalator (m) escalator
Espagne (f) Spain
espagnol Spanish
Espagnol(e) (m/f) Spaniard
espérer to hope
essayer to try, try on
essentiel(le) essential
estragon (m) tarragon
étage (m) floor
état (m) state
États-Unis (m pl) United States
été (m) summer
étiquette (f) label
être (pp été) to be
étudiant(e) (m/f) student
étudier to study
étui (m) case
événement (m) event
éviter to avoid
exagérer to exaggerate
examen (m) exam
excellent excellent
excès (m) excess
excursion (f) excursion
excuser to excuse
excusez-moi excuse me
exercice (m) exercise
expliquer to explain
explorer to explore
extérieur (m) outside
    à l'extérieur on the outside

F

fabriqué made
face: en face de opposite
facile easy
facilité (f) facility
facteur (m) postman
faim (f) hunger
    avoir faim to be hungry
faire (pp fait) to do, make

fait (m) fact
   en fait in fact
famille (f) family
fantastique fantastic
farci stuffed
farine (f) flour
fatigue (f) tiredness
fatigué tired
faut: il faut you/we/I must
faux/fausse false
félicitations (f pl) congratulations
femme (f) woman, wife
femme (f) au foyer housewife
fenêtre (f) window
fer à repasser (m) iron
ferme (f) farm
fermer to close
fermeture éclair (f) zip
fête (f) party
fêter to celebrate
feu (m) fire, heat
feux (m pl) traffic lights
fièvre (f) temperature
fille (f) girl, daughter
film (m) film
fils (m) son
fin (f) end
fin thin, fine
finir to finish
fois (f) time
   à la fois at the same time
foncé dark (colour)
fond (m) back; heart
fonder to found
foot (m) football
forêt (f) forest, woods
formation (f) training, education
formidable amazing
fort strong
four (m) oven
fourni provided
fourrure (f) fur
frais/fraîche chilled
français French
Français(e) (m/f) Frenchman/woman
francophone French-speaking
frère (m) brother

frigo (m) fridge
frisé curly
froid cold
fromage (m) cheese
frontière (f) border
fruit (m) fruit
fruité fruity
fruits secs (m pl) nuts, dried fruit
fumer to smoke

G

gant (m) glove
garçon (m) boy
gare routière (f) bus station
garer to park, to keep in a garage
gastronomie (f) cooking, good food
gastronomique gourmet
gâteau (m) cake
gauche left
   à gauche on/to the left
généralement usually
génial great, cool
genou (m) knee
gentil(le) kind, nice
gentillesse (f) kindness
gîte (m) self-catering holiday home
glacé glossy, shiny
gorge (f) throat
gourde (f) flask
gousse (f) clove (of garlic)
goût (m) taste
goûter (à) to taste
grand big
Grande-Bretagne (f) Great Britain
graphiste (m/f) graphic designer
gratuit free
grave serious
grippe (f) flu
gris grey
gros(se) fat
groupe (m) group
guerre (f) war
guichet de location (m) box office
guide (m/f) guide
guidé guided, accompanied

H

habitant (m) inhabitant
habiter to live
habitude: comme d'habitude as usual
   d'habitude usually
haut high
heure (f) hour, o'clock
heureusement fortunately
heureux/euse happy
hier yesterday
histoire (f) (de l'art) history (of art)
hiver (m) winter
hôpital (m) hospital
horaires d'ouverture (m pl) opening times
hôtel (m) hotel
huile (f) oil
humide humid
hydrothérapie (f) hydrotherapy
hypermarché (m) hypermarket
hypnose (f) hypnosis

I

ici here
idéal ideal
idée (f) idea
identité (f) identity
il y a ago; there is/are
imperméable waterproof
impoli rude
important important
indépandant independent
indice: à fort indice high factor
indiquant indicating
infantile pediatric
infirmier/ière (m/f) nurse
ingénieur (m/f) engineer
   ingénieur chimiste chemical engineer
s'inquiéter to worry
insomnies (f pl) insomnia
institut (m) institute
intempéries (f pl) bad weather
intéressant interesting
intérieur (m) inside
   à l'intérieur on the inside

investissement (m) investment
inviter to invite
ira, irai (from aller) will go
Irlandais(e) (m/f) Irish man/woman
Irlande (f) Ireland
isolé remote
italien(ne) Italian
Italie (f) Italy

J

jaloux/ouse jealous
jamais: ne ... jamais never
jambe (f) leg
Japon (m) Japan
japonais Japanese
jardin (m) garden
jaune yellow
jean (m) pair of jeans; denim
jeu (m) game
joli pretty
jouer to play
jour (m) day
journal (m) newspaper
journaliste (m/f) journalist
journée (f) day
joyeux happy
jumelée: maison jumelée (f) semi-detached house
jumelles (f pl) binoculars
jupe (f) skirt
jusqu'à until, up to
juste just

L

là-bas over there
lac (m) lake
laine (f) wool
laisser to let, leave
laisser cuire to cook
lait (m) milk
lampe (f) lamp, torch
langue (f) language
lapin (m) rabbit
laquelle which one
largeur (f) width
lavable washable
laver to wash
lave-vaisselle (m) dishwasher

lecteur/trice (m/f) reader
léger light, lightweight
Léman: Lac Léman Lake Geneva
lequel/laquelle? which one?
Lettonie (f) Latvia
lettre (f) letter
se lever to get up
libre free
lié linked
lin (m) linen
linge (m) washing
lire (pp lu) to read
liste (f) list
lit (m) bed
lit (m) d'enfant cot
lit (m) simple/double single/double bed
littéraire literary
livre (m) book
local local
location (f) hire (n)
loin far
long(ue) long
le long de along
longueur (f) length
louer to hire
lunettes (de soleil) (f pl) (sun)glasses
luxe (m) luxury

M

machine à laver (f) washing machine
magnétique magnetic
magnifique wonderful
maigre thin
maigrir to lose weight
main (f) hand
maintenant now
maintenir to keep
mais but
maison (f) house
mal (m) ache, pain
avoir mal to be aching
se faire mal to hurt oneself
malade ill
malheureusement unfortunately
Mali (m) Mali
manche (f) sleeve

manger to eat
manque (m) lack
manuel manual (adj)
marcher to walk
mari (m) husband
marié married
se marier to get married
marron brown
matière (f) fabric
matin (m) morning
mauvais bad
mécanicien(ne) (m/f) mechanic
médecin (m/f) doctor
meilleur better, best (adj)
ménage (m) household, housekeeping
mer (f) sea
mère (f) mother
merveilleusement wonderfully
message (m) message
messagerie (f) voice mail
météo (f) weather forecast
mettre to put
mi-chemin: à mi-chemin half-way
micro-ondes (m) microwave oven
Midi (m) South of France
midi midday
mieux better, best (adv)
mignon(ne) sweet, cute
mince slim
ministre (m/f) minister
minute (f) minute
mode (f) fashion
modèle (m) model
modéré moderate
moelleux/euse rich (wine)
moi-même myself
moins less, to (clock time)
mois (m) month
monde (m) world
mondial world (adj)
montagne (f) mountain
monter to climb, go up
montrer to show
morceau (m) piece
motard (m) biker
moulant clingy
mourir (pp mort) to die

moyen(ne) medium
muscade: noix de
muscade (f) nutmeg
musculation (f)
bodybuilding
musée (m) museum
musicien(nne) (m/f)
musician
musique (f) music

N

nager to swim
naissance (f) birth
naître (pp né) to be born
national national
nationalité (f) nationality
naturel(le) natural (adj)
naturellement of course
nautique water (adj)
    les sports nautiques
    water sports
    le ski nautique
    waterskiing
ne ... ni ... ni neither ... nor
nervosité (f) nervousness
neuf/neuve new
    tout neuf brand new
nez (m) nose
niveau (m) level
noir black
noisette hazel (adj)
nom (m) name, surname
nombreux/euse: de
nombreux many,
numerous
nord-est (m) north-east
nouveau/nouvelle new
nouvelles (f pl) news
nuage (m) cloud
nuit (f) night
nul(le) awful
numéro (m) number

O

objectif (m) goal, objective
objet (m) thing, object
obligé obliged
occasion: d'occasion
secondhand
s'occuper de to be busy
with
océan (m) ocean

œil (m) eye
œuf (m) egg
office (m) du tourisme
tourist office
officiellement officially
offrir (pp offert) to offer
oiseau (m) bird
olive (f) olive
on we, you, one
ont (from avoir) (they)
have
opéra (m) opera
opposé: à l'opposé opposite
orage (m) storm
ordinateur (m) computer
ordinateur portable (m)
laptop
ordre: d'ordre of the type
oreille (f) ear
organisateur (m) organiser
organisatrice (f) organiser
organiser to organise
ou or
où where
ouais yeah
oublier to forget
ouest (m) west
outre-mer overseas
ouvrir (pp ouvert) to open

P

pain (m) bread
pantalon (m) trousers
parc (m) park
parce que because
parent (m) parent, relative
parfait perfect
parfaitement perfectly
parler to speak
part: de ma part on my
behalf, from me
partenaire (m/f) partner
participer to take part
partie (f) part
    en partie partly
partir to leave
    à partir de from
pas du tout not at all
passeport (m) passport
passer to spend (time)
passer devant to go past

passion (f) passion
    avoir une passion pour
    to be mad about
passionner to excite, thrill
pauvre (m/f) poor thing
pauvre poor
payer to pay
pays (m) country
Pays-Bas (m pl) Netherlands
Pays de Galles (m) Wales
paysage (m) scenery
pêche (f) fishing
peine: à peine hardly
pendant during
penser to think
perdre to lose
père (m) father
perfection (f) perfection
Pérou (m) Peru
personne (f) person
    ne ... personne nobody
personnel(le) personal
perte (f) loss
petit small
petite-fille (f)
granddaughter
peu a little
    à peu près approximately
peur fear
    avoir peur to be afraid
peut-être perhaps, maybe
peux, peut (from pouvoir)
(I, he/she/it) can
pharmacie (f) chemist's
pharmacien(ne) (m/f)
chemist, pharmacist
phobie (f) phobia
photo (f) photo
physique physical
pièce (f) room
pied (m) foot
    à pied on foot
pincée (f) pinch
pique-nique (m) picnic
piscine (f) swimming pool
piste cyclable (f) cycle
track
pittoresque picturesque
placard (m) cupboard
place (f) room, seat, square
plage (f) beach

plaine (f) plain
plaire to please
  ça me plaît I like it
plaisir (m) pleasure
plan (m) map
planche à voile windsurfing
  faire de la planche à
  voile to go windsurfing
plaque de cuisson (f) hot
plate
plat (m) dish
plein: en plein centre-ville
right in the centre of town
pleut (from pleuvoir)
  il pleut it's raining
plier to bend
plombier (m/f) plumber
pluie (f) rain
plus more
  au plus at most
  de plus en plus more
  and more
  en plus in addition
  ne ... plus no more, no
  longer
plusieurs several
plutôt rather
poche (f) pocket
pochette (f) small pocket
poids (m) weight
pointure (f) shoe size
poivrer to add pepper
poli polite
police (f) police
Pologne (f) Poland
pomme (f) apple
pommier (m) apple tree
pont (m) bridge
  faire le pont make a
  long weekend of it
populaire popular
port (m) port
portable (m) mobile phone
porte-fenêtre (f) French
window
portefeuille (m) wallet
porter to wear, carry
possible possible
pot (m) drink
poulet (m) chicken
pour for
pourquoi why

pourrait (from pouvoir)
could
pouvoir to be able to, can
praticien(ne) (m/f)
practitioner
pratique practical
préféré favourite
préférer to prefer
premier/ière first
prendre to take
prénom (m) first name
préparer to prepare
près (de) near
présenter to introduce
presque almost
prêt ready
prêter to lend
prévu planned, expected
  quelque chose de prévu
  something planned
principal main
prise (f) putting on
privé private
prix (m) price
problème (m) problem
prochain next
proche near
produire to produce
produit (m) product
professeur (m/f) teacher
profiter de to benefit from
profond deep
  la France profonde
  rural France
profondément deeply,
extremely
se promener to go for a
walk
proposer to suggest
propriétaire (m/f) owner
propriété (f) property
protéger to protect
proximité: à proximité
de near
psychique psychological
puis then
pull (m) jumper, pullover
pur pure

Q
qu'est-ce que? what?
qualité (f) quality

quand when
quart (m) quarter
que than
  ne ... que only
quel(le) what, which, what
a ...
quelques some
quelqu'un someone,
anyone
quelque chose something
question (f) question
qui who, which

R
radio (f) radio
raide straight
raison (f) reason
  avoir raison to be right
randonnée (f) hike
rapide rapid
rapidement rapidly
rappeler to remind of
rater to miss
récemment recently
recette (f) recipe
recevoir (pp reçu) to
receive
réchauffement climatique
(m) global warming
recherche (f) research
recommander to
recommend
reconnaissant grateful
rédacteur (m) editor
rédactrice (f) editor
réduction (f) reduction
réduire to reduce
réfrigérateur (m) fridge
refuser to refuse
regarder to watch, look at
région (f) area
régional regional
règlement (m) payment
règne (m) reign
relaxation (f) relaxation
remercier to thank
se remettre en forme to
get fit
remise en forme (f) fitness
remuer to mix, stir
rencontrer to meet

rendez-vous (m) appointment

rénové renovated

renseignements (m pl) information, details

rentrer to return/go home

repas (m) meal

répéter to repeat

répondre to reply

réponse (f) reply

se reposer to relax

réserve naturelle (f) nature reserve

réserver to book, reserve

ressembler to look like

restauré restored

rester to stay, to be left/ remaining

résultat (m) result

retard late

  en retard running late

retirer to withdraw

retraité retired

se retrouver to meet up

retrouver to regain

réunion (f) meeting

se réveiller to wake up

revenir (pp revenu) to come back

reverrai (from revoir) (I) will see again

rhumatismes (m pl) rheumatism

rien: ne ... rien nothing

rigoureux/euse harsh

robuste robust

roman (m) novel

rose (f) rose; pink (adj)

rouge red

royaume (m) kingdom

Royaume-Uni (m) United Kingdom

rue (f) street

russe Russian

Russie (f) Russia

S

sable (m) sand

sac (m) bag

sac à dos (m) backpack, rucksack

sac (m) de sport kit bag

saigner to bleed

sais, sait (from savoir) (I) know, (he/she) knows

saisir to grab

salade (f) salad

saler to add salt

salle (f) hall

salle à manger (f) dining room

salle de bains (f) bathroom

salle de billard (f) billiard room

salle de gym (f) gym

salon (m) living room

salut hi

sans without

santé (f) health

saumon (m) salmon

savoir (pp su) to know

sdb see salle de bains

sec/sèche dry

séjour (m) stay, holiday; living room

  faire un séjour to visit

selon according to

semaine (f) week

sentier (m) footpath

sentiment (m) feeling, wish

séparé separate

sera, serai (from être) will be

sérieux/euse serious

serveur (m) waiter

serveuse (f) waitress

serviette (f) towel, napkin

servir to serve

seul alone

seulement only

si if; yes; so

siècle (m) century

situé situated

ski (m) nautique waterskiing

skier to ski

smoking (m) dinner jacket

snob snobbish

société (f) company

sœur (f) sister

soie (f) silk

soif: avoir soif to be thirsty

soin (m) care

soir (m) evening

soirée (f) evening, evening party

solde: en solde in a sale, at sale price

soleil (m) sun

sombre dark

sommeil (m) sleep

sommes (from être) (we) are

sommet (m) top

sondage (m) survey

sorte (f) sort

sortir to go out, exit

souffrir to suffer

souhaiter to wish

soulager to relieve

source (f) spring, source

sourire to smile

sous under

sous-marin underwater

souvent often

spécialisé specialised

spécialité (f) speciality

sphère (f) sphere

sport (m) sport

sportif/ive sporty

stade (m) stadium

stage (m) course

station (f) resort

  station thermale (f) spa town

stressant stressful

stressé stressed out

streussel (m) strudel

structure (f) structure

sucré sweet

sud (m) south

sud-ouest (m) south-west

Suède (f) Sweden

suffit: ça suffit that's enough

suis (from être) (I) am

Suisse (f) Switzerland

suisse Swiss

Suisse (m/f) Swiss person

suivant following

sujet (m) subject

super great; really

superbe superb

supermarché (m) supermarket

sûr sure

surtout especially

sympa nice

syndicat d'initiative (m) tourist office

système (m) system

T

table (f) table

tableau (m) picture

taille (f) size

tard late

tarif réduit (m) reduction

tarte (f) pie, tart

tee-shirt (m) T-shirt

téléphoner to phone

télévision (f) television

tellement so much

température (f) temperature

temps (m) time; weather
    de temps en temps from time to time

terrain (m) pitch

terrasse (f) terrace

terroir (m) land
    du terroir regional

tête (f) head

TGV (m) TGV *(very fast train)*

théâtre (m) theatre

thérapie (f) therapy

thermalisme (m) spa treatment

thermes (m pl) thermal baths

thermal thermal *(spa)*

thon (m) tuna

timidité (f) shyness

tomate (f) tomato

tomber to fall

tort: avoir tort to be wrong

tôt early

totalement completely

toubib (m) doctor

toujours always

tour (m) measurement *(around something)*; tower

tour: fair le tour de to walk round

touriste (m/f) tourist

tourner to turn

tous all, everyone
    tous les deux both
    tous les jours every day

tousser to cough

tout all, everything
    du tout at all
    tout de suite immediately
    tout le monde everyone

tradition (f) tradition

traditionnel(le) traditional

train (m) train

traitement (m) treatment

tranche (f) slice

tranquille peaceful, quiet

tranquillité (f) peace, calm

travail (m) work

travailler to work

traverser to cross

très very

troisième third

se tromper to make a mistake

trop too

trou (m) hole

trouble (m) trouble

trouver to find

se trouver to be situated

tube (m) tube

turquoise turquoise

U

unique: taille unique one size

université (f) university

utiliser to use

V

vacances (f pl) holidays

va, vais, vas (from aller) go, goes

vaste huge

vélo (m) bike

vélo tout terrain (VTT) mountain bike

vendeur/euse (m/f) sales assistant

vendre to sell

venir (pp venu) to come

vent (m) wind

ventre (m) stomach

véritable real

vers about, towards

verser to pour

vert green

veste (f) jacket

vêtement (m) item of clothing, garment

viande (f) meat

vie (f) life

vierge (f) virgin

vieux/vieille old

vignoble (m) vineyard

vigoureusement vigorously

village (m) village

ville (f) town, city

vin (m) wine

visite (f) visit

visiter to visit

visiteur (m) visitor

vitalité (f) vitality

viticulture (f) wine-growing

vivre to live

vœux: meilleurs vœux (m pl) best wishes

voici here you are

voilà there you are

voile (f) sail
    faire de la voile to go sailing

voir (pp vu) to see

voiture (f) car

vol (m) flight

voler to steal

volley (m) volleyball

volontiers with pleasure

voudrais (from vouloir) (I/you) would like

vouloir (pp voulu) to want

voyage (m) journey

voyager to travel

vrai true

vraiment really

vue (f) view

W

week-end (m) weekend

Y

y there

Z

zippé zipped

English–French glossary

A

about à peu près, environ, vers
to accept accepter
accident accident (m)
according to selon
accountant comptable (m/f)
to ache avoir mal
acidic acidulé
activity activité (f)
actor acteur (m), actrice (f)
to add ajouter
addition (in) en plus
address adresse (f)
to adore adorer
adult adulte (m/f)
advance: in advance à l'avance, d'avance
advert annonce (f)
to advise conseiller
afraid: to be afraid avoir peur
Africa Afrique (f)
after après
afternoon après-midi (m)
age âge (m)
aged âgé
ago il y a
agreed d'accord
airport aéroport (m)
alcohol alcool (m)
Algeria Algérie (f)
all tout
    at all du tout
allergic allergique
allergy allergie (f)
almond amande (f)
almost presque
alone seul
along le long de
Alps Alpes (f pl)
already déjà
also aussi
always toujours
amazing formidable
American américain (adj)
amusing drôle
animal animal (m)
ankle cheville (f)

anybody quelqu'un
apple pomme (f)
apple tree pommier (m)
appointment rendez-vous (m)
approximately à peu près, environ
architect architecte (m/f)
architecture architecture (f)
area région (f)
arm bras (m)
to arrive arriver
artichoke artichaut (m)
as comme
as usual comme d'habitude
athlete athlète (m/f)
Austria Autriche (f)
available disponible
to avoid éviter

B

B&B chambre d'hôte (f)
back dos (m), fond (m)
backpack sac à dos (m)
bad mauvais
baker's boulangerie (f)
balcony balcon (m)
bald chauve
bank banque (f)
bank card carte bancaire (f)
banknote billet (m)
bar bar (m)
bargain aubaine (f)
basil basilic (m)
bath baignoire (f)
to bathe se baigner
bathroom salle de bains (f)
to be être (pp été)
to be able pouvoir (pp pu)
beach plage (f)
to beat battre
beautiful beau, belle
beauty beauté (f)
because parce que
because of à cause de
to become devenir (pp devenu)
bed lit (m)

single/double bed lit simple/double
to go to bed se coucher
bedroom chambre (f)
beef bœuf (m)
before avant
to begin commencer
belt ceinture (f)
bench banc (m)
to bend plier
beneficial bienfaisant
benefit bienfait (m)
to benefit from profiter de
best meilleur (adj), mieux (adv)
    all the best amitiés (f pl), bon courage
    best wishes meilleurs vœux
better meilleur (adj), mieux (adv)
between entre
bicycle vélo (m)
big grand
bike vélo (m)
    mountain bike vélo tout terrain (VTT)
billiard room salle de billard (f)
binoculars jumelles (f pl)
bird oiseau (m)
birth naissance (f)
birthday anniversaire (m)
bit: a bit un peu
bit morceau (m)
black noir
Black Forest Forêt Noire (f)
to bleed saigner
blond blond
blue bleu
boat bateau (m)
bodybuilding musculation (f)
book livre (m)
to book réserver
boot botte (f)
border frontière (f)
to be born naître (pp né)
boss chef (m)
both tous les deux

bottle **bouteille** (f)
bowls **boules** (f pl)
box office **guichet** (m) **de location**
boy **garçon** (m)
Brazil **Brésil** (m)
bread **pain** (m)
bridge **pont** (m)
to bring **apporter**
Britain **Grande-Bretagne** (f)
British **britannique** (adj)
Brittany **Bretagne** (f)
broken **cassé**
brother **frère** (m)
brown **marron, brun**
bruise **bleu** (m), **contusion** (f)
bus **autobus** (m)
bus station **gare routière** (f)
bus stop **arrêt** (m)
busy: to be busy with **s'occuper de**
but **mais**
butter **beurre** (m)
button **bouton** (m)
to buy **acheter**

C

café **café** (m)
cake **gâteau** (m)
calendar **calendrier** (m)
to call **appeler**
called: to be called **s'appeler**
camera **appareil-photo** (m)
campsite **camping** (m)
capital **capitale** (f)
car **voiture** (f)
to carry **porter**
case **étui** (m); **cas**
    in any case **en tout cas**
cashmere **cachemire** (m)
cashpoint **distributeur** (m) **de billets**
castle **château** (m)
to celebrate **fêter**
central heating **chauffage central** (m)
century **siècle** (m)
certainly **bien sûr**
change **changement** (m)
to change **changer, échanger**
cheese **fromage** (m)

chemical engineer **ingénieur chimiste** (m/f)
chemist **pharmacien(ne)** (m/f)
chemist's **pharmacie** (f)
cherry **cerise** (f)
cherry tree **cerisier** (m)
chicken **poulet** (m)
child **enfant** (m/f)
chilled **frais**
chimney **cheminée** (f)
Chinese **chinois** (adj)
chocolate **chocolat** (m)
choice **choix** (m)
to choose **choisir**
church **église** (f)
cider **cidre** (m)
cinema **cinéma** (m)
city **ville** (f)
class **classe** (f)
classmate **camarade** (m/f) **de classe**
climate **climat** (m)
to climb **monter**
clingy **moulant**
to close **fermer**
clothes **vêtements** (m pl)
cloud **nuage** (m)
clove (of garlic) **gousse** (f) **(d'ail)**
coast **côte** (f)
coffee **café** (m)
cold **froid**
collar **collier** (m)
colleague **collègue** (m/f)
colour **couleur** (f)
to come **venir**
to come back **revenir** (pp **revenu)**
comfort **confort** (m)
comfortable **confortable**
to communicate **communiquer**
company **société** (f)
compartment **compartiment** (m)
compass **boussole** (f)
compatible **compatible**
completely **complètement, totalement**
computer **ordinateur** (m)
conference (academic) **colloque** (m)
confidence **confiance** (f)

congratulations **félicitations** (f pl)
to contact **contacter**
to contain **contenir**
contents **contenu** (m)
continent **continent** (m)
to continue **continuer**
conversation **conversation** (f)
to cook **cuire** (pp **cuit), laisser cuire**
cooked **cuit**
cookery **cuisine** (f)
corner **coin** (m)
Corsica **Corse** (f)
to cost **coûter**
cot **lit d'enfant** (m)
cotton **coton** (m)
to cough **tousser**
country **pays** (m); **campagne** (f)
countryside **campagne** (f)
couple **couple** (m)
course **cours** (m), **stage** (m)
course: of course **bien sûr, naturellement**
cousin **cousin(e)** (m/f)
covered **couvert**
credit card **carte** (f) **de crédit**
to cross **traverser**
crossroads **carrefour** (m)
to crush **écraser**
cupboard **placard** (m)
curly **frisé**
to cut **couper**
cycle track **piste cyclable** (f)

D

to dance **danser**
dangerous **dangereux**
dark **foncé** (*colour*); **sombre**
dark-haired **brun**
date **date** (f)
to date **dater**
daughter **fille** (f)
daughter-in-law **belle-fille** (f)
day **jour** (m), **journée** (f)
dear **cher/chère**
to decide **décider (de)**
deep **profond**
degree **degré** (m)
delegate **délégué** (m)

delicate **délicat**
delicious **délicieux/euse**
denim **jean (m), en jean**
department **département (m)**
deposit **arrhes (f pl)**
depression **dépression (f)**
to describe **décrire**
desert **désert (m)**
designer **créateur/trice (m/f)**
dessert **dessert (m)**
detail **détail (m), renseignement (m)**
to die **mourir (pp mort)**
different **différent**
dining room **salle à manger (f)**
dinner **dîner (m)**
to have dinner **dîner**
dinner jacket **smoking (m)**
director **directeur/trice (m/f)**
disappointed **déçu**
to discover **découvrir**
to discuss **discuter**
disgusting **dégoûtant**
dish **plat (m)**
dishwasher **lave-vaisselle (m)**
divorced **divorcé**
to do **faire**
doctor **médecin (m/f), docteur (m), toubib (m)**
dog **chien (m)**
drink **pot (m)**
to drink **boire (pp bu)**
dry **sec/sèche**
duration **durée (f)**
during **pendant**

E

each **chaque**
each person **chacun**
eagle **aigle (m)**
ear **oreille (f)**
early **tôt**
east **est (m)**
easy **facile**
to eat **manger**
ecology **écologie (f)**
editor **rédacteur (m), rédactrice (f)**
effective **efficace**
egg **œuf (m)**

elderly **âgé**
electric **électrique (adj)**
electrical goods **électro-ménager (m)**
elegant **élégant**
employee **employé(e) (m/f)**
end **bout (m), fin (f)**
engineer **ingénieur (m/f)**
England **Angleterre (f)**
English **anglais(e) (adj);** *(language)* **anglais (m);** *(person)* **Anglais(e)**
to enjoy oneself **s'amuser**
enough **assez**
    that's enough **ça suffit**
to enter **entrer**
entirely **entièrement**
environment **environnement (m)**
equipped **équipé**
escalator **escalator (m)**
especially **surtout**
essential **essentiel(le)**
estate agent **agent immobilier (m)**
estate agent's **agence immobilière (f)**
evening **soir (m), soirée (f)**
event **événement (m)**
every **chaque**
every day **tous les jours**
everyone **tous, tout le monde**
to exaggerate **exagérer**
exam **examen (m)**
to exceed **dépasser**
excellent **excellent**
excess **excès (m)**
to exchange **échanger**
excursion **excursion (f)**
to excuse **excuser**
excuse me **excusez-moi**
exercise **exercice (m)**
to exit **sortir**
expensive **cher/chère**
to explain **expliquer**
to explore **explorer**
eye **œil (m) (pl yeux)**

F

fabric **matière (f), tissu (m)**
facility **facilité (f)**
fact **fait**
    in fact **en fait**

to fall **tomber**
false **faux/fausse**
family **famille (f)**
famous **célèbre, connu**
to fancy *(want)* **avoir envie de**
fantastic **fantastique**
far **loin**
farm **ferme (f)**
fashion **mode (f)**
fat **gros(se)**
father **père (m)**
favourite **préféré**
to feel like **avoir envie de**
film **film (m)**
to find **trouver**
finger **doigt (m)**
to finish **finir**
fire **feu (m)**
fireplace **cheminée (f)**
first **premier/ière**
first (of all) **d'abord**
first name **prénom (m)**
fishing **pêche (f)**
fit: to get/keep fit **se remettre en forme**
fitness **remise en forme (f)**
flask **gourde (f)**
flat **appartement (m)**
flight **vol (m)**
floor **étage (m)**
flour **farine (f)**
flu **grippe (f)**
fog **brouillard (m)**
following **suivant**
foot **pied (m)**
    on foot **à pied**
football **foot (m)**
footpath **sentier (m)**
for **pour; depuis**
forest **forêt (f)**
to forget **oublier**
former **ancien(ne)**
fortunately **heureusement**
free **gratuit; libre**
freezer **congélateur (m)**
French **français (adj);** *(language)* **français (m);** *(person)* **Français(e) (m/f)**
French window **porte-fenêtre (f)**
French-speaking **francophone**

fridge **frigo** (m),
réfrigérateur (m)
friend **ami(e)** (m/f),
copin(e) (m/f)
from **de, à partir de**
front: in front **à l'avant**
     in front of **avant**
fruit **fruit** (m)
fruity **fruité**
full **complet/complète**
funny **drôle**
fur **fourrure** (f)

G

game **jeu** (m)
garden **jardin** (m)
garlic **ail** (m)
garment **vêtement** (m)
gentle **doux/douce**
German **allemand** (adj);
(*language*) **allemand** (m);
(*person*) **Allemand(e)** (m/f)
Germany **Allemagne** (f)
to get off **descendre**
to get up **se lever**
girl **fille** (f)
to give **donner**
glasses **lunettes** (f pl)
glossy **glacé**
glove **gant** (m)
to go **aller**
to go down **descendre**
to go for a walk **se
promener**
to go home **rentrer**
to go out **sortir**
to go to bed **se coucher**
to go up **monter**
goal **objectif** (m)
good **bon(ne)**
granddaughter **petite-fille**
(f)
graphic designer **graphiste**
(m/f)
grateful **reconnaissant**
Great Britain **Grande-
Bretagne** (f)
great **génial, classe, super**
green **vert**
grey **gris**
group **groupe** (m)
guide **guide** (m/f)
gym **salle de gym** (f)

H

hair **cheveux** (m pl)
hairdresser **coiffeur** (m),
coiffeuse (f)
half **demi(e)**
     half past **et demie**
     half-way **à mi-chemin**
hall **salle** (f)
hand **main** (f)
to happen **arriver**
happiness **bonheur** (m)
happy **heureux/euse,
joyeux/euse**
hardly **à peine**
harsh **rigoureux/euse**
hat **chapeau** (m)
to have **avoir**
to have to **devoir, il faut**
hazel **noisette** (adj)
head **tête** (f)
health **santé** (f)
to hear **entendre**
to heat **chauffer**
heating **chauffage** (m)
hello **bonjour, allô** (*on
phone*)
helmet **casque** (m)
to help **aider**
here **ici**
here you are **voici**
hi **salut**
high **haut**
hike **randonnée** (f)
hill **colline** (f)
hire **location** (f)
to hire **louer**
history (of art) **histoire** (f)
(de l'art)
holiday **séjour** (m)
holiday camp **colonie de
vacances** (f)
holidays **vacances** (f pl)
to hope **espérer**
horse riding **équitation** (f)
hospital **hôpital** (m)
hot **chaud**
hot plate **plaque de
cuisson** (f)
hotel **hôtel** (m)
hour **heure** (f)
house **maison** (f)
     at the house of **chez**
housewife **femme au
foyer** (f)

how **comment**
how many **combien (de)**
huge **vaste**
humid **humide**
hungry: to be hungry **avoir
faim**
to hurt oneself **se faire mal**
husband **mari** (m)

I

idea **idée** (f)
ideal **idéal**
identity card **carte** (f)
d'identité
if **si**
ill **malade**
immediately **tout de suite**
important **important**
in **à, en, dans**
independent **indépendant**
information
renseignements (m pl)
inhabitant **habitant** (m)
inside **intérieur** (m)
     on the inside **à l'intérieur**
institute **institut** (m)
interesting **intéressant**
interview **entretien** (f)
to introduce **présenter**
investment **investissement**
(m)
to invite **inviter**
Ireland **Irlande** (f)
Irish **irlandais** (adj);
(*language*) **irlandais** (m);
(*person*) **Irlandais(e)** (m/f)
iron **fer à repasser** (m)
Italian **italien(ne)** (adj);
(*language*) **italien** (m);
(*person*) **Italien(ne)** (m/f)
Italy **Italie** (f)

J

jacket **veste** (f)
Japan **Japon** (m)
Japanese **japonais** (adj);
(*language*) **japonais** (m);
(*person*) **Japonais(e)** (m/f)
jealous **jaloux/ouse**
jeans **jean** (m)
journalist **journaliste** (m/f)
journey **voyage** (m)
jumper **pull** (m)
just **juste**

K

to keep maintenir
kettle bouilloire (f)
key clé (f)
kind gentil(le)
kindness gentillesse (f)
kiss bisou (m)
kit bag sac (m) de sport
kitchen cuisine (f)
knee genou (m)
to know (fact) savoir;
(person, place) connaître
known connu

L

label étiquette (f)
lack manque (m)
lake lac (m)
   Lake Geneva lac Léman
lamp lampe (f)
language langue (f)
laptop ordinateur (m)
portable
large grand
last dernier
to last durer
late tard, en retard
laundry linge (m)
leaflet dépliant (m)
to learn apprendre
to leave laisser; partir
left gauche
   on/to the left à gauche
to be left rester
leg jambe (f)
lemon citron (m)
to lend prêter
length longueur (f)
less moins
to let laisser
letter lettre (f)
level niveau (m)
life vie (f)
lift ascenseur (m)
light (colour) clair; (weight)
léger
to like aimer
   I like it ça me plaît
linen lin (m)
lining doublure (f)
list liste (f)
to listen écouter

little petit
   a little un peu
to live habiter, vivre
living room salon (m),
séjour (m)
local local
long long(ue)
longer: no longer ne ... plus
to look at regarder
to look for chercher
to look like ressembler
to lose perdre
loss perte (f)
lost property report
déclaration (f) de perte
lot: a lot (of) beaucoup
(de)
lover amoureux (m)
to lower baisser
luck chance (f)
lucky: to be lucky avoir de
la chance
lunch déjeuner (m)
to have lunch déjeuner
luxury luxe (m)

M

mad: to be mad about
avoir une passion pour
made fabriqué
magnetic magnétique
main principal
to make faire
many beaucoup (de), de
nombreux/euse
map carte (f), plan (m)
married marié
to get married se marier
martial arts arts martiaux
(m pl)
to match coordonner
maybe peut-être
meal repas (m)
meat viande (f)
   cold meats charcuterie (f)
mechanic mécanicien(ne)
(m/f)
medium moyen(ne) (adj)
to meet rencontrer, se
retrouver
meeting réunion (f)
message message (m)
microwave oven micro-
ondes (m)

midday midi
milk lait (m)
mineral water eau
minérale (f)
minister ministre (m/f)
minute minute (f)
mistake: to make a mistake
se tromper
to mix remuer
mobile phone portable (m)
model modèle (m)
moderate modéré
money argent (m)
month mois (m)
more plus
   more and more de plus
   en plus
morning matin (m)
most (le/la) plus
   at most au plus
mother mère (f)
mountain montagne (f)
mountain bike vélo (m)
tout terrain (VTT)
mouth bouche (f)
mud boue (f)
museum musée (m)
music musique (f)
musician musicien(ne)
(m/f)
must: to have to il faut,
devoir
myself moi-même

N

name nom (m)
   first name prénom (m)
national national
nationality nationalité (f)
natural naturel
nature reserve réserve
naturelle (f)
near près (de); proche (adj)
neck cou (m)
to need avoir besoin de
neither ... nor ne ... ni ... ni
Netherlands Pays-Bas
(m pl)
never ne ... jamais
new nouveau/nouvelle,
neuf/neuve
news nouvelles (f pl)
newspaper journal (m)
next prochain, suivant

next to à côté de
nice aimable, gentil(le), sympa
night nuit (f)
nobody ne ... personne
north nord (m)
north-east nord-est (m)
nose nez (m)
nothing ne ... rien
novel roman (m)
now maintenant
number numéro (m)
nurse infirmier/ère (m/f)
nutmeg noix de muscade (f)
nuts fruits secs (m pl)

O

o'clock heures (f pl)
obliged obligé
ocean océan (m)
to offer offrir (pp offert)
office bureau (m)
officially officiellement
often souvent
oil huile (f)
OK d'accord
old vieux/vieille, ancien(ne)
olive olive (f)
only seulement, ne ... que
to open ouvrir
opening times horaires (m pl) d'ouverture
opera opéra (m)
opinion avis (m)
    in my opinion à mon avis
opposite en face de
to order commander
to organise organiser
organiser organisateur (m), organisatrice (f)
other autre
outside extérieur
    on the outside à l'extérieur
outskirts alentours (m pl), environs (m pl), banlieue (f)
oven four (m)
over there là-bas
overseas outre-mer
owner propriétaire (m/f)

P

pain douleur (f)
painful douloureux/euse
painkiller analgésique (m)
pair couple (m)
parent parent (m)
park parc (m)
part partie (f)
partly en partie
partner compagnon (m), compagne (f), partenaire (m/f)
party fête (f), soirée (f)
to pass passer
    to go past passer devant
passport passeport (m)
to pay payer
peace (and quiet) calme (m), tranquillité (f)
peaceful tranquille
to peel éplucher
pepper poivre (m)
perfect parfait
perfection perfection (f)
perfectly parfaitement
perhaps peut-être
person personne (f)
personal personnel(le)
Peru Pérou (m)
pharmacist pharmacien (m), pharmacienne (f)
phone appareil (m), téléphone (m)
to phone appeler, téléphoner
photo photo (f)
physical physique
picnic pique-nique (m)
picture tableau (m)
picturesque pittoresque
pie tarte (f)
piece morceau (m)
pinch pincée (f)
pink rose
pitch terrain (m)
pity: it's a pity c'est dommage
place endroit (m)
plain plaine (f)
to plan compter
to play jouer
pleasant agréable
to please plaire

pleased to meet you enchanté
pleasure plaisir (m)
plumber plombier (m/f)
pocket poche (f)
police police (f)
police officer agent (m/f) de police
police station commissariat (m) (de police)
polite poli
poor pauvre
    poor thing le/la pauvre (m/f)
popular populaire
port port (m)
possible possible
post office bureau de poste (m)
postman facteur (m)
to pour verser
practical pratique
practitioner praticien(ne) (m/f)
to prefer préférer
pregnant enceinte
to prepare préparer
present cadeau (m)
press officer attaché(e) de presse (m/f)
pretty joli
price prix (m)
private privé
problem problème (m)
to produce produire
product produit (m)
property propriété (f)
to protect protéger
provided fourni
psychological psychique
pullover pull (m)
pure pur
to put mettre

Q

quality qualité (f)
quarter quart (m)
question question (f)
quiet tranquille
quite assez

R

rabbit lapin (m)
radio radio (f)
railway chemin de fer (m)
rain pluie (f)
to rain pleuvoir
rapid rapide
rather plutôt
to reach atteindre
to read lire (pp lu)
reader lecteur (m), lectrice (f)
ready prêt
real véritable
really absolument, super, vraiment
reason raison (f)
to receive recevoir (pp reçu)
recently récemment
recipe recette (f)
to recommend recommander, conseiller
red rouge
to reduce réduire
reduction réduction (f), tarif réduit (m)
to refuse refuser
regional régional, du terroir
relative parent (m)
to relax se reposer
relaxation relaxation (f)
to relieve soulager
to remain rester
to remind rappeler
remote isolé
renovated rénové
to repeat répéter
reply réponse (f)
to reply répondre
to report an incident faire une déclaration
research recherches (f pl)
to reserve réserver
resort station (f)
restaurant brasserie (f), restaurant (m)
restored restauré
result résultat (m)
retired retraité
to return rentrer, retourner

rheumatism rhumatismes (m pl)
rich (food/drink) moelleux/moelleuse
right droite
    on/to the right à droite
to be right avoir raison
road route (f)
robust robuste
room pièce (f), place (f)
    at room temperature chambré
rose rose (f)
rucksack sac à dos (m)
rude impoli
Russia Russie (f)
Russian russe (adj); (language) russe (m); (person) Russe (m/f)

S

to sail faire de la voile
salad salade (f)
sale: for sale à vendre
sales soldes (m pl)
    at sale price en solde
sales assistant vendeur (m), vendeuse (f)
salmon saumon (m)
salt sel (m)
sand sable (m)
saucepan casserole (f)
sauerkraut choucroute (f)
to say dire (pp dit)
scenery paysage (m)
school collège (m), école (f)
Scotland Écosse (f)
sea mer (f)
seaside bord (m) de la mer
season ticket carte d'abonné, carte d'abonnement
seat place (f)
second deuxième
secondhand d'occasion
to see voir
to see again revoir
see you soon à bientôt
to sell vendre
semi-detached house maison jumelée (f)
to send envoyer
separate séparé

serious grave, sérieux/euse
to serve servir
several plusieurs
sheet drap (m)
shirt chemise (f)
short court
shoulder épaule (f)
to show montrer
shower douche (f)
shower (of rain) averse (f)
silk soie (f)
since depuis
singer chanteur (m), chanteuse (f)
sister sœur (f)
to sit down s'asseoir
situated situé
to be situated se trouver
size taille (f) (clothes), pointure (f) (shoes)
to ski faire du ski
skirt jupe (f)
sleeve manche (f)
slice tranche (f)
slim mince
to slim maigrir
small petit
to smile sourire
to smoke fumer
snobbish snob
so si
sofa bed canapé-lit (m)
some quelques; en
somebody quelqu'un
something quelque chose
son fils (m)
sorry désolé
sort sorte (f)
South America Amérique (f) du Sud
south sud (m)
South of France Midi (m)
south-west sud-ouest (m)
spa station thermale (f)
Spain Espagne (f)
Spaniard Espagnol(e) (m/f)
Spanish espagnol (adj); (language) espagnol (m); (person) Espagnol(e) (m/f)
to speak parler
specialised spécialisé
speciality spécialité (f)
speech discours (m)
to spend (time) passer

spinach épinards (m pl)
sport sport (m)
sports centre complexe sportif (m)
sporty sportif/ive
square place (f)
stable écurie (f)
stadium stade (m)
starter entrée (f)
state état (m)
stay séjour (m)
to stay rester
to steal voler
to stir remuer
stomach ventre (m)
to stop arrêter, s'arrêter
storm orage (m)
straight raide
straight ahead tout droit
street rue (f)
stressed stressé
stressful stressant
strong fort
student étudiant(e) (m/f)
to study étudier
stuffed farci
subject sujet (m)
to suffer souffrir
to suggest proposer
suit costume (m)
to suit aller, convenir
summer été (m)
sun soleil (m)
sun cream crème solaire (f)
to sunbathe bronzer
sunglasses lunettes de soleil (f pl)
sunny interval éclaircie (f)
supermarket supermarché (m)
sure sûr
surname nom (m)
survey sondage (m)
swap échange (m)
sweet mignon(ne); sucré
to swim nager, se baigner
swimming pool piscine (f)
Swiss suisse (adj), (person) Suisse (m/f)
Switzerland Suisse (f)
system système (m)

T

table table (f)
tablet comprimé (m)
to take prendre
to take part participer
tarragon estragon (m)
taste goût (m)
to taste goûter (à)
tasting dégustation (f)
teacher professeur (m/f)
television télévision (f)
temperature fièvre (f), température (f)
terrace terrasse (f)
terrible affreux/euse
than que
to thank remercier
that ça, cela; ce
that one celui-là (m), celle-là (f)
theatre théâtre (m)
then ensuite, puis
therapy thérapie (f)
there y, là
   over there là-bas
therefore donc
there is, there are il y a
there you are voilà
thin maigre, fin
thing objet (m)
to think penser
third troisième
thirsty: to be thirsty avoir soif
this ce, cette
this one celui-ci (m), celle-ci (f)
throat gorge (f)
ticket billet (m)
time fois (f), temps (m)
   from time to time de temps en temps
tired fatigué
tiredness fatigue (f)
today aujourd'hui
together ensemble
tomato tomate (f)
tomorrow demain
too aussi; trop
tooth dent (f)
top sommet (m); débardeur (m) (sleeveless)
torch lampe (f)

tourist office office du tourisme (m), syndicat d'initiative (m)
tourist touriste (m/f)
towards vers
towel serviette (f)
town centre centre-ville (m)
town ville (f)
tradition tradition (f)
traditional traditionnel(le)
traffic lights feux (m pl)
train train (m)
trainers baskets (m pl)
trainer entraîneur (m)
to travel voyager
treatment (spa) cure (f), traitement (m)
trouble trouble (m)
trousers pantalon (m)
true vrai
to try (on) essayer
T-shirt tee-shirt (m)
tuna thon (m)
to turn tourner
turquoise turquoise

U

under sous
to understand comprendre (pp compris)
underwater sous-marin
unfortunately malheureusement
United Kingdom Royaume-Uni (m)
United States États-Unis (m pl)
university université (f)
unpleasant désagréable
until jusqu'à
up to jusqu'à
to use utiliser
usual: as usual comme d'habitude
usually généralement, d'habitude

V

vacuum cleaner aspirateur (m)
very très, super
view vue (f)
village village (m)

vineyard vignoble (m)
visit visite (f)
to visit visiter, faire un
séjour
visitor visiteur (m)
volleyball volley (m)

W

to wait (for) attendre
waiter serveur (m)
waitress serveuse (f)
to wake up se réveiller
Wales Pays de Galles (m)
to walk marcher
to go for a walk se
promener
walk round fair le tour de
walking shoes chaussures
de marche (f pl)
wallet portefeuille (m)
to want vouloir
war guerre (f)
warm chaud
to wash laver
washable lavable
washing linge (m)
washing machine machine
à laver (f)
to watch regarder
water eau (f)
water skiing ski nautique
(m)
waterproof imperméable
water sports sports
nautiques (m pl)
to wear porter
weather temps (m)
weather forecast météo (f)
wedding anniversary
anniversaire (m) de
mariage
week semaine (f)
weekend week-end (m)
weight poids (m)
welcome bienvenue
well bien; alors; enfin
well-being bien-être (n)
west ouest (m)
what? qu'est-ce que?
quel(le)?
when quand
where où
which quel(le); qui; que

which one? lequel/
laquelle?
white blanc/blanche
white coffee café (m) au
lait
who qui
whole entier/ière
why pourquoi
width largeur (f)
wife femme (f)
wind vent (m)
window fenêtre (f)
windsurfing: to go
windsurfing faire de la
planche à voile
wine vin (m)
winter hiver (m)
to wish souhaiter
  best wishes meilleurs
  vœux
with avec
  with pleasure volontiers
to withdraw retirer
without sans
woman femme (f)
wonderful magnifique
woods forêt (f)
wool laine (f)
work travail (m)
to work travailler
world monde (m)
world mondial (adj)
to worry s'inquiéter
to write écrire
wrong: to be wrong avoir
tort

Y

year an (m), année (f)
yellow jaune
yesterday hier
yet encore
youth hostel auberge de
jeunesse (f)

Z

zip fermeture (f) éclair
zipped zippé